DATE			
OCT 18 1997			
MAR 03 2000			
SEP 05 2000			

LIVING BY
FICTION

OTHER BOOKS BY ANNIE DILLARD

Holy the Firm
Pilgrim at Tinker Creek
Tickets for a Prayer Wheel

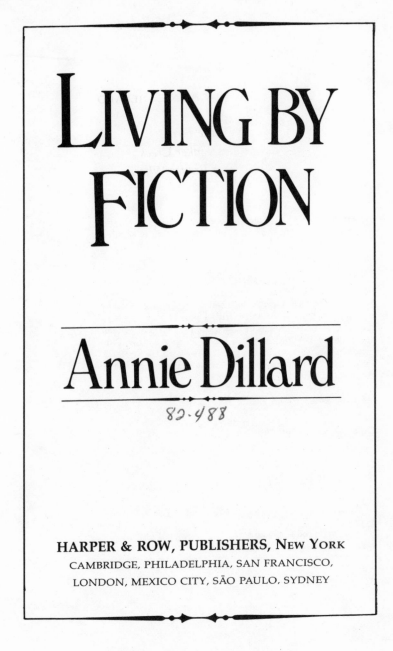

LIVING BY FICTION

Annie Dillard

HARPER & ROW, PUBLISHERS, New York

CAMBRIDGE, PHILADELPHIA, SAN FRANCISCO,
LONDON, MEXICO CITY, SÃO PAULO, SYDNEY

Excerpts from this book have appeared in *Harper's Magazine, Massachusetts Review*, and *Twentieth Century Literature*.

FIRST EDITION

Designer: Gloria Adelson

Library of Congress Cataloging in Publication Data
Dillard, Annie.
  Living by fiction.

  1. Fiction—20th century—History and criticism.
2. Fiction. I. Title.
PN3503.D5 1982   809.3'04   81-47882
ISBN 0-06-014960-4   AACR2

---

82 83 84 85 86 10 9 8 7 6 5 4 3 2 1

This book is dedicated to people whose names are, for the most part, unknown to me. They are men and women across the country who love literature and give it their lives: who respect literature's capacity to mean, who perhaps teach, who perhaps write fiction or criticism or poetry, and who above all read and reread the world's good books. These are people who, if you told them the world would end in ten minutes, would try to decide—quickly—what to read.

Those known to me are only a small sampling. There is my friend Judy Hawkes, who works in New York as a messenger "boy." There is Robert Fitzgerald—much-honored poet and translator of Homer—and Penny Lawrans, at Harvard and Yale respectively. This book is for them—a woman I know well and a couple I met briefly—who live by the same love for literature; and for R. C. Day at Humboldt State University in Arcata, California (the briefest acquaintance with whom prompted this dedication); for L. L. Lee at Western Washington University in Bellingham, Washington, John R. Moore and Betty Moore at Hollins College in Virginia, and Paul Horgan at Wesleyan University in Connecticut; for Michael Collins in New York, Daniel Butterworth in North Carolina, Doe Burn in California, Cort Conley on Waldron Island, Washington; for Garrett Epps and Spencie Love at large, the late DeVene Harrold in Florida, Ruth Vande Kieft in New York, Julia Randall in Maryland,

and Jim McCulloch in Texas; for all of you in university English departments or in hock (or both), people well known or unknown, tending bar or retired, going to night school, raising children, writing novels or criticism, fitting pipes, awarding or receiving degrees—who love books, think about books, read or write books, for love of literature. I wish I could name all of you, all of you in every country and township in the land; for I know by extrapolation that you are there.

Contents

Acknowledgments

I am most especially and fondly grateful to L. L. Lee, Phyllis Rose, Gary Clevidence, and Rose Moss, who encouraged and challenged me so generously; to Ed Rubacha, Joan Jurale, Susan Magovern, Shirley Henn, and Louis Mink, who helped track sources; to the Ossabaw Foundation and Wesleyan University, which granted me time and space; and to Mary Connie Comfort, who fed the cats.

Art must recreate, in full consciousness,
and by means of signs, the total life
of the universe, that is to say, the soul
where the varied dream we call the universe
is played.

—Teodor de Wyzewa, 1886

Introduction

This is, ultimately, a book about the world. It inquires about the world's meaning. It attempts to do unlicensed metaphysics in a teacup. The teacup at hand, in this case, is contemporary fiction.

Why read fiction to think about the world? You may, like most of us most of the time, read fiction for other things. You may read fiction to enjoy the multiplicity and dazzle of the vivid objects it presents to the imagination; to hear its verbal splendor and admire its nimble narrative; to enter lives not your own; to feel, on one hand, the solemn stasis and immutability of the work as enclosed art object—beginning and ending the same way every time you read it, as though a novel were a diagram inscribed forever under the vault of heaven—and to feel, on the other hand, the plunging force of time compressed in its passage, and that compressed passage like a river's pitch crowded with scenes and scenery and actions and characters enlarged and rushing headlong down together.

You may, I say, enjoy fiction for these sensations, and turn to nonfiction for thought.

This is, indeed, a wonderful way to live. You read biography, ethics, cultural anthropology, psychology if you can stand it, aesthetics, linguistics, art criticism, every kind of personal narrative imaginable, and history above all, history of peoples and ideas and knowledge and places, history of everything. You read theology if such is your bent, and contemporary metaphysics if you can find any. And you turn to science for data, in order to do your own thinking; you read physics and astronomy, geography, cellular biology, field zoology and botany—the works. This is entertaining: "Let us gather facts," Buffon said, "in order to have ideas." If you do this, you will have ideas about facts.

You can, in short, lead the life of the mind, which is, despite some appalling frustrations, the happiest life on earth. And one day, in the thick of this, approaching some partial vision, you will (I swear) find yourself on the receiving end of—of all things—an "idea for a story," and you will, God save you, start thinking about writing some fiction of your own. Then you will understand, in what I fancy might be a blinding flash, that all this passionate thinking is what fiction is about, that all those other fiction writers started as you did, and are laborers in the same vineyard.

Fiction can deal with all the world's objects and ideas together, with the breadth of human experience in time and space; it can deal with things the limited disciplines of thought either ignore completely or destroy by methodological caution, our most pressing concerns: personality, family, death, love, time, spirit, goodness, evil, destiny, beauty, will.

Fiction writers are, I hope to show, thoughtful interpreters of the world. But instead of producing interpretations—instead of doing research or criticism—they doodle on the walls of the cave. They make art objects which must themselves be interpreted. How convolute, how absurd, how endlessly interesting is this complexity! The world is filling up with works of fiction, with these useless, beautiful objects of thought—to what end? What links any work of fiction with anything we want to learn? To the world we see? To our understanding of the world we see? Does fiction illuminate the great world itself, or only the mind of its human creator?

Like many people, I have for years been reading fiction by various United States and South American writers like Vladimir Nabokov, John Barth, Robert Coover, Thomas Pynchon, Jorge Luis Borges, Julio Cortázar, Carlos Fuentes, and Gabriel García Márquez, and by European writers like Samuel Beckett, the dull Alain Robbe-Grillet, the wonderful Italo Calvino. I have asked myself how their work's goals differ from those of the Modernists before them—Faulkner, Joyce, Mann, Kafka, say—or from the goals of Hardy or Eliot, or of Saul Bellow or Salinger or Mailer. What do these varied contemporary writers above—the contemporary modernists—have to say about the world? About fiction? What characterizes their fictional worlds and their artistic methods? The answers to these questions are old hat among critics. Nevertheless,

these considerations, and some interesting side issues—
like the matter of integrity in art—occupy Part One of
this three-part book.

In Part Two, which is far more entertaining, I ask why
this brand of contemporary fiction does not wholly dominate the field. Why is anyone still writing traditional fiction? Why has there been no radical revolution in fiction?
How far can fiction go in the direction of abstraction?
How do fiction's audience, its publishers, and even its
critics, influence its direction? These are, I think, lively
topics. There is also in this section a chapter about a
much-beloved side issue, contemporary prose styles.

The final third of the book raises the roof on fiction
and takes on the world at large. Who, among thinkers, is
interpreting the great world itself—landscape and culture
together—in terms of human meaning? Is interpretation
possible at all? We lock in asylums people who see meaning in clouds and rocks, but we heap honors on people
who see meaning in children's jokes and patterns
scratched on pots. Where do those of us who are not in
asylums draw the line—by tacit agreement—between the
humanly meaningful and meaningless? Is the search for
meaning among the high heaps of the meaningless a
fool's game? Is it art's game? What is (gasp) the relationship between the world and the mind? Is *knowledge* possible? Do we ever discover meaning, or do we always
make it up?

I approach fiction, and the world, and these absurdly
large questions, as a reader, and a writer, and a lover.
Although my critical training and competence, such as it
is, is as a careful textual critic, I have here flung this sensible approach aside in favor of enthusiasm, free specula-

tion, blind assertion, dumb joking, and diatribe. The book as a whole sees the mind and the world as inextricably fitted twin puzzles. The mind fits the world and shapes it as a river fits and shapes its own banks.

MIDDLETOWN, CONNECTICUT
MAY 1981

PART ONE

Some Contemporary Fiction

CHAPTER 1

Fiction in Bits

Many contemporaries write a fiction intended to achieve traditional kinds of excellence. Many others write a fiction which is more abstracted—the kind of fiction Borges wrote in *Ficciones,* or Nabokov wrote in *Pale Fire.* This latter kind of fiction has no name, and I do not intend to coin one. Some people call it "metafiction," "fabulation," "experimental," "neo-Modernist," and, especially, "Post-Modernist"; but I find all these terms misleading. "Post-Modernist" is the best, but it suffers from the same ambiguity which everyone deplores in its sibling term, "Post-Impressionist."

Recently a stranger from New York City sent me a green button, a big green button, which read: POST-MODERNIST. From his letter I inferred that he disliked Modernism, found it baffling and infuriating, and for reasons I could not fathom, included me on his team.

But Modernism is not over. The historical Modernists are dead: Kafka, Joyce, Faulkner, and also Biely, Gide, Malraux, Musil, Woolf. But one could argue—and I do—that diverse contemporary writers are carrying on, with new emphases and further developments, the Modernists' techniques.

I am going to use the dreadful mouthful "contemporary modernist" to refer to these contemporary writers and their fiction. I trust that the clumsiness of the term will prevent its catching on. I will also use the lowercase, nonhistorical term "modernist" loosely, to refer to the art of surfaces in general. The historical Modernists explored this art and bent it, in most cases, to surprisingly traditional ends. Transitional writers like Knut Hamsun, Witold Gombrowicz, and Bruno Schulz expanded its capacity for irony. Now various contemporaries are pushing it to various interesting extremes: Jorge Borges, Vladimir Nabokov, Samuel Beckett, and Robert Coover, John Barth, John Hawkes, William Burroughs, Donald Barthelme, Thomas Pynchon, Rudolph Wurlitzer, Thomas M. Disch, Alain Robbe-Grillet, Jonathan Baumbach, William Hjorstberg, and Flann O'Brien, Italo Calvino, Tommaso Landolfi, Julio Cortázar, Manuel Puig, Elias Canetti, and Carlos Fuentes.

Time in Smithereens

Nothing is more typical of modernist fiction than its shattering of narrative line. Just as Cubism can take a roomful of furniture and iron it onto nine square feet of canvas, so fiction can take fifty years of human life, chop it to bits, and piece those bits together so that, within the limits of the temporal form, we can consider them all at once. This is narrative collage. The world is a warehouse of forms which the writer raids: this is a stickup. Here are the narrative leaps and fast cuttings to which we have become accustomed, the clenched juxtapositions, interpenetrations, and temporal enjambments. These techniques are standard practice now; we scarcely remark them. No degree of rapid splicing could startle an audience raised on sixty-second television commercials; we tend to be bored without it. But to early readers of Faulkner, say, or of Joyce, the surface bits of their work must have seemed like shrapnel from some unimaginable offstage havoc.

The use of narrative collage is particularly adapted to various twentieth-century treatments of time and space. Time no longer courses in a great and widening stream, a stream upon which the narrative consciousness floats, passing fixed landmarks in orderly progression, and growing in wisdom. Instead, time is a flattened landscape, a land of unlinked lakes seen from the air. There is no requirement that a novel's narrative bits follow any progression in narrative time; there is no requirement that the intervals between bits represent equal intervals of elapsed time. Narrative collage enables Carlos Fuentes in *Terra Nostra* to approximate the eternal present which is his subject. We read about quasars one minute; we enter an elaborated scene with Pontius Pilate the next. Narrative collage enables Grass in *The Flounder* to bite off even greater hunks of time and to include such disparate elements as Watergate, the history of millet, Vasco da Gama, a neolithic six-breasted woman, and recipes for cooking eel. Narrative collage enables Charles Simmons, in *Wrinkles*, artistically to fracture a human life and arrange the broken time bits on the page. And it enables Michael Ondaatje, a Canadian novelist, to include in his novel *The Collected Works of Billy the Kid* not only prose narration in many voices and tenses, but also photographs ironic and sincere, and blank spaces, interviews, and poems.

Joyce, 163 years after Sterne, started breaking the narrative in *Ulysses*. The point of view shifts, the style shifts; the novel breaks into various parodies, a question-and-answer period, and so forth. Later writers have simply pushed farther this notion of disparate sections. They break the narrative into ever finer particles and shatter time itself to smithereens. Often writers call attention to the particles by giving them each a separate chapter, or number, or simply a separate title, as Gass does in "In the Heart of the Heart of the Country." Donald Barthelme has a story ("The Glass Mountain") in which each sentence constitutes a separate, numbered section. All these cosmetics point to a narration as shattered, and as formally ordered, as a Duchamp nude.

If and when the arrow of time shatters, cause and effect may vanish, and reason crumble. This may be the point. I am thinking here of Robert Coover's wonderful story "The Babysitter," in which the action appears as a series of bits told from the point of view of several main characters. Each version of events is different and each is partially imaginary; nevertheless, each event triggers other events, and they all converge in a final scene upon whose disastrous particulars the characters all of a sudden agree. No one can say which causal sequence of events was more probable. Time itself is, as in the Borges story, a "garden of forking paths." In other works of this kind, events do not trigger other events at all; instead, any event is possible. There is no cause and effect in Julio Cortázar's *Hopscotch*, an unbound novel whose pages may be shuffled. There is no law of noncontradiction in Barthelme's story "Views of My Father Weeping." Barthelme writes the story in pieces, half of which examine a father's death and half of which depict the father, in the same time frame, alive and weeping.

Narrative collage, and the shifting points of view which accompany it, enable fiction to make a rough literature of physics, a better "science fiction" which acknowledges the equality of all relative positions by assigning them equal value. One extreme of this kind of fiction is an art without center. The world is an undirected energy; it is an infinite series of random possibilities. (Barthelme ends "Views of My Father Weeping" with a section which reads only "Etc.") The world's coherence derives not from a universal order but from any individual stance. God knows this is a common enough position. It is not really physics but ordinary relativism. (In literature, relativism need not be cynical; in "The Babysitter " and *Hopscotch* it is downright gleeful. Relativism is particularly suited to artists and writers, who, as a class, have often been dedicated to private vision anyway, and especially to the private vision of the world as a storehouse of manipulable ideas and things.)

Not only does time shift rapidly in contemporary modernist narrative; so does everything else. Space, for instance, is no longer a three-dimensional "setting"—the great house into which generations of little lords are born, the setting into which readers sitting in their own great houses can settle. Instead, space is, or may be, a public, random, or temporary place. Instead of being exotic, places may be merely alien—rucks in the global fabric where no one is at home. The action may occur all over the globe, with everywhere the same narrative distance, so that works of this sort (*V., Terra Nostra*) may have geographical breadth without emotional depth. (I am not speaking pejoratively here in the least; I mean merely to distinguish between sets of excellences.) The traditional novelist labors to render an exotic setting familiar, to put us at our ease in the Alps or at home in burning Moscow. But contemporary writers may flaunt their multiple, alien settings, as Pynchon does, or make of the familiar world someplace alien and strange, as Thomas M. Disch does with Manhattan. Narrative collage touches every aspect of the fiction in which it appears. The point of view shifts; the prose style shifts and its tone; characters turn into things; sequences of events abruptly vanish. Images clash; realms of discourse bang together. Zeus may order a margarita; Zsa Zsa Gabor may raise the siege of Orléans. In a recent *TriQuarterly* story, Heathcliff meets Chateaubriand on a golf course. These things have almost become predictable.

The use of narrative collage, then, enables a writer to recreate, if he wishes, a world shattered, and perhaps senseless, and certainly strange. It may emphasize the particulate nature of everything. We experience a world unhinged. Nothing temporal, spatial, perceptual, social, or moral is fixed.

This is the fiction of quantum mechanics; a particle's velocity and position cannot both be known. Similarly, it may happen that in the works of some few writers, the narrative itself cannot be located. Events occur without discernible meaning; "mere anarchy is loosed upon the world." What if the world's history itself, and the events of our own lives in it, were as jerked, arbitrary, and fundamentally incoherent as is the sequence of episodes in some contemporary fictions? It is, these writers may say; they are.

The Egg in the Cage

I would like to pause here to talk about artistic integrity. Distinctions of value need to be made among contemporary modernist works, as among all works, and I think they can be made most pointedly here, where technique fades into meaning and raises the issue of integrity.

Interestingly enough, contemporary modernist fiction, unlike traditional fiction, has no junk genres. Like poetry so long as it is serious, fiction, so long as it is witty, is almost always assumed to be literature. Well, then, it has already passed the qualifying rounds and must go on to the finals: Does it have meaning? For any art, including an art of surface, must do more than dazzle. Is this art in the service of idea? And it is right here that *some* contemporary modernist fiction can claim, Yes, it does mean; it recreates in all its detail the meaninglessness of the modern world. And I cry foul. When is a work "about" meaninglessness and when is it simply meaningless?

Clearly the shattering of what we feel as the rondure of experience (or of what, according to this theory, we who were born after 1911 have never felt as the rondure of experience), and the distant and ironic examination of the resultant fragments, serve, in Robbe-Grillet's terms, "to exile the world to the life of its own surface"—and, by extension, to express our sense of exile on that surface. If meaning is contextual, and it is, then the collapse of ordered Western society and its inherited values following

World War I cannot be overstressed; when we lost our context, we lost our meaning. We became, all of us in the West, more impoverished and in one sense more ignorant than pygmies, who, like the hedgehog, know one great thing: in this case, why they are here. We no longer know why we are here—if, indeed, we are to believe that large segments of European society ever did. At any rate, our contemporary questioning of why we are here finds a fitting objective correlative in the worst of the new fictions, whose artistic recreation of our anomie, confusion, and meaninglessness elicits from us the new question, Why am I reading this?

We judge a work on its integrity. Often we examine a work's integrity (or at least I do) by asking what it makes for itself and what it attempts to borrow from the world. Sentimental art, for instance, attempts to force preexistent emotions upon us. Instead of creating characters and events which will elicit special feelings unique to the text, sentimental art merely gestures toward stock characters and events whose accompanying emotions come on tap. Bad poetry is almost always bad because it attempts to claim for itself the real power of whatever it describes in ten lines: a sky full of stars, first love, or Niagara Falls. An honest work generates its own power; a dishonest work tries to rob power from the cataracts of the given. That is why scenes of high drama—suicide, rape, murder, incest—or scenes of great beauty are so difficult to do well in genuine literature. We already have strong feelings about these things, and literature does not operate on borrowed feelings.

As in the realm of feeling, so in the realm of intellect. Naming your characters Aristotle and Plato is not going to make their relationship interesting unless you make it so on the page; having your character shoot himself in the end does not mean that anyone has learned anything; and setting your novel in Buchenwald does not give it moral significance. Now: may a work of art borrow meaning by being itself meaningless? May it claim thereby to have criticized society? Or to have recreated our experience? May a work claim for itself whole hunks of other people's thoughts on the flimsy grounds that the work itself, being so fragmented, typifies our experience of this century? Can a writer get away with this? I don't think so.

But let me state the question more sympathetically, from the writer's point of view. The writer's question is slightly different. If the writer's honest intention is to recreate a world he finds meaningless, must his work then be meaningless? If he writes a broken book, is he not then a bad artist? On the other hand, if he unifies a world he sees as shattered, is he not dishonest? All this is an old problem for any writer, for a traditional one as well as a contemporary one. Stated broadly, the question is, What is negative art? What can it be? What can a writer do when his intention is to depict seriously a boring conversation? Must he bore everybody? How should he handle a dull character, a hateful scene? (Everyone knows how the hated voice of a hated character can ruin a book.) Or, in the big time, how can a writer show, as a harmonious, artistic whole, times out of joint, materials clashing, effects without cause, life without depth, and all history without meaning?

There are several strategies which may ameliorate these difficulties. A writer may make his aesthetic surfaces very, very good and even appealing, in the hope that those surface excellences will impart to the work enough positive value, as it were, to overwhelm its negativity. Better, he may widen his final intention to include possibilities for meaning which illuminate, without relieving, suffering: but this solution, the writing of tragedy or of contemporary art whose intentions are wider than those posited, does not address the problem. The only real solution is this, which obtains in all art: the writer makes real artistic meaning of meaninglessness the usual way, the old way, by creating a self-relevant artistic whole. He produces a work whose parts cohere. He imposes a strict order upon chaos. And this is what most contemporary modernist fiction does. Art may imitate anything but disorder. The work of art may, like a magician's act, pretend to any degree of spontaneity, randomality, or whimsy, so long as the effect of the whole is calculated and unified. No subject matter whatever prohibits a positive and unified handling. After all, who would say of "The Waste Land" that it is meaningless, or of *Molloy*, or *Mrs. Bridge?* We see in these works, and in traditional black works like Greene's *Brighton Rock* and Lowry's *Under the Volcano*, the unity which characterizes all art. In this structural unity lies integrity, and it is integrity which separates art from nonart.

Let me tread shaky ground in order to insert a note from René Magritte on this business of integrity. Any juxtaposition may be startling. Narrative collage is a cheap source of power. An onion ring in a coffin! Paul of Tarsus and Shelly Hack! We can all do this all day. But in the juxtaposition of images, as in other juxtapositions, there is true and false, says Magritte. Magritte says we know birds in a cage. The image gets more interesting if we have, instead of a bird, a fish in the cage, or a shoe in the cage; "but though these images are strange they are unhappily accidental, arbitrary. It is possible to obtain a new image which will stand up to examination through having something final, something right about it: it's the image showing an egg in the cage."

Now, what do we make of this curious assertion of Magritte's, that surrealist images may be right or wrong? What can be right about a surrealist image? I am certainly not going to endorse as an artistic criterion Magritte's vague, emotional phrase "something right about it." But I do endorse his notion that the right image will "stand up to examination." After all, there is nothing too mysterious about the rightness of an egg's replacing a bird. The two have met. In other words, the "something right" which "will stand up to examination" is ordinary unity. Notice that Magritte's surrealism by no means intends to traffic in "accidental" or "arbitrary" images. He uses these words to damn. Must arbitrariness always be damning? Must it forever be out of bounds not as a subject but as a technique? I think so.

Let me insert here a regret that criticism has no other terms than "device" and "technique" for these deliberate artistic causes which yield deliberate artistic effects. In painting and in music, the word "technique," at least, has a respectable sound; but in fiction, and especially to laymen, both "device" and "technique" sound sinister, as though writers were cold-blooded manipulators and gadgeteers who for genius substitute a bag of tricks. They are; of course they are. But the trick is the work itself. The trick is intrinsic. One does not produce a work and then give it a twist by inserting devices and techniques here and there like acupuncture needles. The work itself is the device. In traditional fiction the work is device made flesh; in contemporary modernist fiction the work may be technique itself or device laid bare.

All this is not to say that the fragmentation of the great world is the only theme of narrative collage: far from it. These techniques—abrupt shifts, disjunctive splicings and enjambments of time, space, and voice—are common coin. Almost all contemporary writers, including writers of traditional fiction, use them toward any number of different ends. For that matter, the historical Modernists themselves used them for various, often traditional ends. In Joyce's *Ulysses*, in Faulkner's *The Sound and the Fury*, the use of segmented narrative deepens the reader's sense of the fictional world and its complex characters and scenes. The technique serves the works' other themes, as it does in Garrett's *Death of the Fox*, Ellison's *Invisible Man*, Lessing's *The Golden Notebook*, and Durrell's *Alexandria Quartet*. And even when a work's theme is fragmentation, the work may itself be unified, and the fragmentation may not be bad news; James and many other writers have celebrated the world's "blooming, buzzing confusion."

Note, then, that the fragmentation of narrative line may be, and usually is, as formally controlled as any other aspect of fiction. There is nothing arbitrary whatsoever about fragmentation itself. In fact, as a technique it may elicit *more* formal control than a leisured narrative technique which imitates the thickened flow of time in orderly progression, if only because it requires the writer clearly to identify the important segments of his work and skip the rest. No charming narrative dalliances prevent our seeing his scenes as parts of a whole; no emotional coziness lulls our minds to sleep.

The virtues of contemporary modernist fiction are literary, are intellectual and aesthetic. They are the solid excellences of complex, formally ordered pattern. Most contemporary modernist fiction, and the best of it, does not claim these virtues *and* the incidental virtues of realistic fiction as well. You do not find Calvino promoting "verisimilitude"; you do not read Nabokov as a document of the times. This is as it should be. I bring up the question of integrity here only because it is here that a writer may most readily fool himself—always an attractive possibility. On one hand, sophisticated, hurried readers continue to judge works on the sophistication of their surfaces. On the other hand, our culture continues to pay lip service to the incidental and dull virtues of realism. So a writer may combine the two sets of excellence inappropriately. He may fool himself into reproducing the broken, sophisticated-looking forms of good contemporary modernist fiction without its unified content, in the hope that the narrative technique, *as an end in itself*, has an intrinsic significance. It not only looks good, it is "realistic." It is "social criticism." He may fool himself into shirking the difficult, heartbreaking task of structuring a work of art on the grounds that art is imitation (all of a sudden) and a slapdash fiction imitates a seriously troubled world.

But I am exaggerating, and speaking here more in theory than in fact. I am pummeling an unnamed straw man, a straw author, who composes, like Dadaist Tristan Tzara, by stirring a hatful of scraps. I am certainly not thinking here of a great writer like Cortázar, or Coover. In fact, I know for certain of no such writer of fiction, and I'm afraid I would not name one if I did. Serious writers are not consciously dishonest. I mean only to mutter darkly that in the present confusion of technical sophistication and significance, an emperor or two might slip by with no clothes.

Anyone with wit and training can search a work for

sense. And sense is by no means an obsolete virtue: sense, and not the skill to dazzle, is the basal criterion for art. Surface obscurity is, of course, by no means a sign of its absence. On the contrary, such obscurity usually proves to be smoke from some wonderfully interesting fire. We simply must not mistake the smoke for the fire. I am certain that much, if not most, of today's lasting fiction derives from contemporary modernist writers of integrity (writers like Nabokov, Borges, Beckett, Barth, Calvino). That other writers may produce fictional surfaces similar to theirs, but without their internal integrity, does not in any way dim their achievement. But someone must distinguish between art and mere glibness.

All we need are responsible readers who demand real artistic coherence from a work. And we need book reviewers who understand how literature works and do not forget their training when they read a dust jacket. After all, new, subtle, and intellectualized forms of sense demand, and must continue to produce, detailed critical effort. We need much more serious textual criticism of contemporary work—work to whose formal intentions publishers and reviewers are usually indifferent—and we need a wide forum for such criticism. It's a pity it's so dull. Nevertheless, such effort gave us Wallace Stevens and Nabokov; it must continue, undaunted by fluff, to ocate the great work being produced today. (Or the philistines will get us, or the paperbacks won't.)

Let me conclude this excursus with a few bald assertions. Meaninglessness in art is a contradiction in terms. Meaning in art is contextual. What does a whale mean? A whale means whatever an artist can make it mean in a given work. Art is the creation of coherent contexts. Since words necessarily refer to the world, as paint does not, literary contexts must be more responsible to the actual world than painting contexts must be. That is, it is easily conceivable that a painted blue streak should represent a ship's hull in one painting and a curved arm in another. But that fictional element in *Moby-Dick* had better be a whale or something mighty like one. The blue streak can hold up its end of the artistic structure in virtually any context, but whales belong at sea. Writers do not create whales; whales are known and given; you can only do so much with them. You would be hard put in your serious novel to make a whale stand for a repressive Middle Eastern regime, or baseball, or agriculture. You would violate the bonds of unity if you tried to force a serious narrative connection between a vicious whale and, say, Isabel Archer. It would be precious to yoke them together without just cause. It would be mere comedy. It would be painting a shoe in the cage.

In all the arts, coherence in a work means that the relationship among parts—the jointed framework of the whole—is actual, solid, nailed down. (Of course, a proper demonstration of valid connection among parts would require a full-scale exegesis of a text, an interruption which I am unwilling to suffer. There are solid readings of standard works. Reliable readings of intelligent lyric poetry usually demonstrate the relationship of parts very clearly, if only because the texts at hand are so small. I could refer the reader to, say, Bloom or Ellman on Yeats, Frye on Blake, Vendler or Sukenick on Stevens. In contemporary fiction, the *Hollins Critic* essays such as those collected in *The Sounder Few* give intelligent exegeses of contemporary texts.) In all the arts, coherence and integrity go hand in hand. One cannot toss onto one's canvas a patch of blue paint and hope one's friends like it or some clever critic finds a reason for it. Similarly, one cannot add the weight of idea to a piece of fiction by setting a whale swimming through it, or by inserting Adolf Hitler with a larding needle, or by scrambling the world's contents with a pen.

Contemporary modernist fiction, in fact, requires *more* coherence than traditional fiction does. For one of the things this new fiction does is bare its own structure. (How long a novel would *Pale Fire* be in the hands of Thomas Mann?) This fiction sees that the formal relationship among parts is the essential value of all works of art. So it strips the narration of inessentials: like Hugo's excursions into the history of all aspects of human culture, like the unities of time, space, and action, like emotion. It bares instead its structural bones, as *Pale Fire* does, and *Invisible Cities,* and *Ficciones;* it bares its structural bones, brings them to the surface, and retires. Those bones had better be good. If a writer is going to use forms developed by intelligent people, he should use them intelligently. It does not do to mimic results without due process. Traditional fiction has the advantage here, I think. In a conservative work well fleshed, we may not notice at once that the joints do not articulate, nor the limbs even meet the torso. There may in fact be so much flesh that the parts cohere as it were bonelessly. But it is easy to see, if we look, taped joints on a skeleton.

It is interesting that John Fowles rewrote *The Magus. The Magus* is in many ways a contemporary modernist piece of fiction—in its fantastic transfigurations, its object-like and grotesque characters, and its emphasis on the irrational. But the first edition of *The Magus*—now it can be told—was dishonest work, the relationship of whose parts was pleaded. Its structure collapsed at a touch. It is interesting that Fowles rewrote it because, I fancy, Fowles understood that in order to make his bid as an important writer he needed to set his house in order and redress his crimes against integrity.

At best, integrity and intelligence go hand in hand to ensure against laziness, false analogies, pleaded connections, and sleight of word. Integrity demands of intelligence that it forge true connections on the page. Intelligence calls for integrity for the challenge of it, and from intelligent respect for the audience of literature, and respect for the art of literature itself, and for its capacity to mean.

CHAPTER 2

Two Wild Animals, Seven Crazies, and a Breast

Character

Contemporary modernist characters are extraordinary. Gone are the men and women of Dickens, say, or Hugo, whose exteriors are familiar to everyone, whose interiors are explored and forgiven by their authors. Also absent are characters who brood earnestly, and who seek God or the good or wisdom or love or, for that matter, money. We no longer examine the interior lives of characters much like ourselves. Instead, we watch from afar a caravan of alien grotesques in, as it were, big hats. Remedios the Beauty, in *One Hundred Years of Solitude*, is typical. She carries about with her a noisy bag of her parents' bones, is followed by butterflies, and is assumed bodily into heaven from her bath. In García Márquez, as in Pynchon, we see characters from a great distance, as colorful and extraordinary objects.

Oddly enough, grotesque modernist characters are more apt to be telling the story than not. Their first-person narration persuasively engages us with them, odd as they are, while it separates us a notch from the actual action. On this tension, and on the tension between sympathy for and estrangement from their weird characters, depends much that is interesting in modernist fiction. We are yanked into some remarkable sympathies. Gone are the trustworthy days of Trollope, the clear-headed days of Defoe, in which the author sat us down and told us a story. Now our first-person narrators are not authors: we are doing very well if they are even people. Instead they are cows, mental defectives, toddlers, dinosaurs, paranoid schizophrenics, dying cripples, breasts, axolotls, Neanderthals, or goats (Agee, "A Mother's Tale"; Faulkner, *The Sound and the Fury*; Grass, *The Tin Drum*; Calvino, *Cosmicomics*; Tommaso Landolfi, "Week of Sun"; Beckett, *Malone Dies*; Roth, *The Breast*; Cortázar, "Axolotl"; Gardner, *Grendel*; Barth, *Giles Goat-Boy*).

Contemporary modernist writers flatten their characters by handling them at a great distance, as if with tongs. They flatten them narratively. They flatten them, as Robbe-Grillet does, by treating them as sense objects alone, as features of landscape. A writer may show his characters' speeches and actions without the faintest trace of motivation, so that we watch the scenes as strangers, as if we were freshly air-dropped into Highland, New Guinea. The speeches and actions of such characters seem random, unwilled, or absurdist. The narrator of Witold Gombrowicz's *Ferdydurke*, for instance, wants desperately to run out of a classroom, but instead sticks his finger in his shoe and complains, Beckett-like, "You cannot run with one finger at floor level."

A writer may comment on his characters or, as Barth does, mock them. He may give them funny names which call attention to the artificiality of the whole business: Humbert Humbert, Betty Bliss, Word Smith. He may give them names which call attention to ideas, either ironically or in earnest: Oedipa Maas, Benny Profane, and J. Henry Waugh (=JHVH, Jahweh). (In two cases, at least, a writer wishes a name to be a double entendre, but no one pronounces the name as he intended, so the effect vanishes. Barth originally pronounced the Giles of *Giles Goat-Boy* with a hard *g*, punning on "guile," but when the book became known as *"Jiles" Goat-Boy*, Barth gave up his own pronunciation and joined the crowd. Nabokov fancied, rather endearingly, that the name Ada as spoken would coincide with the proper pronunciation of the word "ardor"—as indeed it may, somewhere. At any rate, guile and ardor are the respective subjects of the two novels.)

Other contemporary characters are historical; thus a writer playfully violates his fictional frame by giving us Nixon or Henry Ford. In an L. L. Lee story, Borges appears as a nineteenth-century writer of naturalist fiction, "the Argentine Dreiser." Also contemporary is the return of the picaro, a fairly flat character whose story is episodic. The contemporary picaresque novel is by no means necessarily modernist—*A Cool Million, Under the Net, The Adventures of Augie March, Lucky Jim, The Ginger Man, Little Big Man*—but their picaros reflect the general flattening of character.

In the traditional novel, the eighteenth- and nineteenth-century European novel, "character" means man or woman in society. Central characters in the Stendhal novel, the Dickens novel, the James novel, interest themselves in blood, money, and advancement to an extent that is simply staggering to anyone who approaches literature through formal methods appropriate to modernism. Where is the art? Where is the metaphysics? These characters, and presumably their authors as well, are more interested in a man's cash assets than in his bargainings with eternity. Conflict in such novels seldom, if ever, erupts between people and whales. At the European novel's close, characters do not, as in the American novel, ride off alone into the sunset. Instead, they are drawn off together in carriages to the bank.

Today all this is gone, even in naturalist fiction. Before the Romantic revolution, characters try to advance themselves; after it, they try to save themselves. Historical modernist characters, like Joe Christmas in *Light in August*, like Kafka characters and the nameless characters in *Hunger* and *Invisible Man*, are a lonely lot. They try to keep body and soul together despite society, instead of trying to propel their bodies in ever more expensive garments through it. And contemporary modernist characters are not interested in society at all. Their sphere of activity is the novel. To Beckett characters, Borges characters, Nabokov characters, society does not exist. They may lack hearts as well as social ambition. They are no more lonely than chessmen. At any rate, the jolly picaros, and Calvino's Cosimo, who lives in trees, and the various axolotls, dinosaurs, cows, etc., which I have mentioned, have on their minds other things than marrying money.

Such characters tend to be less human simulacra, less rounded complexities of deep-seated ties and wishes, than focal points for action or idea. Pynchon people are lines of force. Some Nabokov characters are literally chessmen. Borges characters may be ideas. They are not ideas represented by people-like characters, as in the "novel of ideas" such as *The Plague,* in which the Doctor, representing Scientific Reason, goes about acting scientifically reasonable and voicing Scientific Reason's opinion of everything; instead, Borges characters are ideas considered as objects for contemplation: Funes the Memorious on his deathbed, an idea in a sheet, more referred to than present, or Pierre Menard, absent altogether. Later Borges characters, on the other hand, are again lines of force, mythic and wholly externalized objects whose roles are identical with their definitions: the bandit robs, the overseer whips, the gunslinger slings guns. It would be ludicrous if anyone saw these characters as trapped in roles for which they are personally unsuited. In the world of surfaces, human reality coincides with social appearance.

Traditional characters are "rounded," or "modeled," or "drawn in depth." The very terms are spatial analogues. Such characters are a Renaissance invention analogous to painting's deep space. The art of representing the world is the art of depth. Modernist art, in painting and in fiction, is the art of surfaces. It no longer seeks to imitate nature in the round; it no longer seeks a technique which dissolves invisibly "down" into the depths of things. It seeks instead what might be called a new perspective, the careful flattening of forms on the surface in such a way that the depths of things float "up" into technique. Characters' role in this fiction is formal and structural. Their claim on us is not emotional but intellectual. They are no longer fiction's center.

The role of character has shrunk to such a degree that

in some contemporary works, especially stories, there are no characters at all: in Ursula K. Le Guin's excellent story "The Author of the Acacia Seeds and Other Extracts from the *Journal of the Association of Therolinguistics*," for instance, and in Stanislaw Lem's collection *A Perfect Vacuum*, and in many Borges stories, such as "The Library of Babel," "Pierre Menard, Author of Don Quixote," and "A New Refutation of Time."

Point of View

The twentieth-century development in fiction of a thoroughly limited point of view has been overemphasized, I think, especially in the light of more radical recent developments. One could argue that the use of a limited point of view is positively old-fashioned. When Conrad, Joyce, Faulkner, and Woolf used strictly limited points of view, they were moving the novel's arena into the mind and voice of individuals. This is consonant with the traditional virtues of depth, of rounded character, of emotional intimacy, and of sincerity. Nevertheless, you could also argue, and I shall, that the intimate voice of a narrator moves fiction a notch toward its own surface, and as such is new-fashioned indeed. Paradoxically, such an intimate, limited point of view actually distances us from the action.

It is, after all, the phenomenal world which is literature's subject, and a given character is but one of many phenomena. A character's limited consciousness and his obtrusive voice erect a veil between us and things and between us and the forgetfulness which is total immersion. Marlow's oldhandedness does not match our innocence of the horrifying particulars he relates. Hearing his ironic voice may strengthen the severity of our judgment of events, but it does not deepen our experience of them. We are not meant to experience them. We are meant to contemplate them.

Marlow's interrupting voice also deepens our admiration for Conrad's narrative technique. That is, it is an artifice which intermittently calls attention to itself. So also, *a fortiori*, is the obtrusive and disjunctive surface treatment of Molly Bloom's maundering mind. It is an aesthetic experience, not an intimate one. Do we enter her world? her mind? or that section of *Ulysses?* A tour de force is, after all, a power play; we gasp, but we do not weep. Finally, a narrator's personality tinges his record of events and inclines us to skepticism. And skepticism is no traditional virtue; it is the beginning of the end, of the shattering of the world of things and its ultimate dispersal into bits from which to make worlds of mind.

When several voices take turns telling a story—a device common in Faulkner, most clearly seen in *As I Lay Dying*—their effect compared to that of a single voice is even more distancing. The use of such multiple voices inclines us to relativism with respect to fictional events on one hand and toward aesthetic appreciation with respect to the artwork on the other. And when these several voices each iterate the same event, like the blind men describing the elephant, in such a way that the flow of time halts while everybody steps off and looks around (*Light in August, The Sound and the Fury*), the effect is more distancing yet. For while we as audience walk round and round some fictional event, that event, while it acquires rondure and depth before our eyes, also becomes isolated. Cut off from the rush of time and the direct flow of unconsidered sense data, a given reiterated event—say, Luster's loss of his quarter in *The Sound and the Fury*—becomes a fixed and immobile artistic or intellectual object. When we hear each of the blind men in turn, the hearsay elephant itself seems to us more and more remote. It becomes less an experienced event than an object of speculation. It becomes quite patently an element of fiction, a focal point of artistic structure.

And so these comparatively recent uses of limited points of view may in fact be contemporary modernist in their effects. They diminish our emotional involvement in the tale and draw attention to the teller. Those limited viewpoints which are very limited or obtrusive—those which are unintelligent, out of position, alien, grotesque, or fanatical—add to the work a layer of irony, like an oblique plane. When a tale's teller is an axolotl or a dinosaur or a breast, we scarcely enter his tale with wholehearted sympathy, although we may be drawn to the character himself. So works with such narrators (Cortázar, "Axolotl"; Calvino, *Cosmicomics*; Roth, *The Breast*) move us by paradox, as Cubist canvases do. Their odd voices and viewpoints deepen our involvement in what would traditionally be considered the works' more or less invisible *surface*, the tale's teller. Yet at the same time they flatten what would traditionally be the deep part of the work, the tale itself. And so by making the deep parts shallow and the shallow parts deep, they bring to the work an interesting and powerful set of tensions, like Cubist intersecting planes.

Similarly, limited points of view emphasize the isolation of individual consciousness. When that individual is grotesquely limited, they suggest the grotesquerie of any limited stance; they stress the bias and partiality of anyone's knowledge. By moving fiction's arena from the material world to consciousness itself, they stress modern *self*-consciousness, and suggest a world in which total and forgetful immersion in events is no longer possible.

Often, as in Coover's "The Babysitter" and in *As I Lay Dying*, the points of view collide, mingle, or switch. In these cases, the point of view is simply another aspect of narrative collage, and expresses its themes. Not only is the world in bits, but our senses are parceled out among us. We are forced to be skeptics and relativists. The number of narrators of a given event may be multiplied indefinitely. The world is that which cannot be known. The world is that which we each imagine. What, in "The Babysitter," really happened? The world is caught in a crossfire between necessity and possibility; the world is the fabrication of a billion imaginations all inventing it at once.

Return to Narration

The intrusion of the author into his own book is part of narrative collage. The author pops in and interrupts his story's flow with confiding, ironic, or extravagant comment.

The device is not new. Trollope and Fielding insert themselves into their novels at regular intervals to warn, lecture, or praise their characters or their readers, or to disclaim any responsibility for characters' misbehavior, or otherwise to strike quondam attractive moral postures. Their intention is in part traditional, then; they seek to engage us in their works' moral depths, such as they are. And they seek, in lesser part, something of what Sterne sought: but Sterne was two centuries ahead of his time. They seek, that is, to slip us the wink. The novel is a game or a joke shared between author and reader. When a writer like Barth speaks up in his fiction today, he returns to Sterne, he parodies the eighteenth-century novel, and he makes a virtue of his own self-consciousness. Barth parodies his self-consciousness too, brilliantly: he even celebrates the self-awareness of the writer whose chosen art is so developed and all its possibilities so known that he cannot enter into it forgetfully.

Now as in the eighteenth century, a novel's chapters may open with an authorial précis of their contents: this parodies not only the older usage, but also contemporary advertising copy. (Chapter 21 of Spanish writer Manuel Scorza's novel *Drums for Rancas* is headed "Where, Free of Charge, the Tireless Reader Will Watch Dr. Montenegro Grow Pale." This sort of irony in contemporary fiction represents the neotenous and monotonous retention of adolescent humor into adult life.)

A writer may interrupt his narration not only with his voice but also with his disconcerting presence. Borges appears in his own work as a mythical intelligence. Nabokov graces his own novels as a figure—a figure at once majestic and ironic, the way Alfred Hitchcock appears in his own films. All these interruptions and cameo appearances celebrate the art of it all; they remind us that we are as it were in a theater, and that the narrative itself is a conscious and willed artifice.

Finally, if telling a good story engages readers, then it stands to reason that you can effectively *distance* readers by telling a bad story. Say what you will of *Finnegans Wake*, it is a lousy story. So are Beckett novels, most Robbe-Grillet novels, recent Stanislaw Lem novels, and countless short stories of which early Borges fictions are the type.

Certain of the most attractive elements of good story-telling—I mean what blurbs call rip-roaring good story-telling—have been taken over by films and popular fiction. We think of a "walloping" good story as having a little death in it, and possibly some elemental forces like fire or the sea, and likely some big battles, crossed romances, exotic settings, betrayals, switched babies, murders, fortune or treasure, international intrigue, escapes, missed letters, vows, or disguises. All this drama and action appeals to practically everybody; the very popular genres depend on it; literary novels now avoid it. The serious novelist takes pains to distinguish his work from trash. If popular films and popular novels have good stories, then literary novels shall not. If despite all your precautions your novel is epic in scale, if it embodies such quaint narrative virtues as enlargement and diversity of action, forcefulness of dramatic conflict, vivid spectacle, and heart-pounding suspense, someone will accuse you of writing with an eye toward a film sale. No one will like you anymore.

Even among the serious writers of traditional fiction, dramatic storytelling went out with World War I. I do not know if Freud made the difference, or the very grave and very colorless events of the century itself; but at some point, the poeple in novels stopped galloping all over the countryside and started brooding from chairs. Everything became psychological and interiorized. External conflict became internal tension. We swallowed the arena and can no longer watch the show. Internal battles lack color. You may search the novels of Virginia Woolf in vain for so much as a single horse.

Narration, then, in the name of purity, can go the way of character. It is optional. It is suspect: recently Richard

Lingeman, writing in *The New York Times*, accused the ending of a novel of being "plotty." Narration is finally dispensable. "To tell a story," Robbe-Grillet proclaims from his corner, "has become strictly impossible." Of course, Robbe-Grillet is speaking from his own theory. Telling a story is not at all impossible if the writer wants to; but for contemporary modernist writers, it is getting increasingly impossible to want to. At any rate, there are forms of fiction in which no story is told at all. These are usually short stories whose specialized forms forbid both characters and narration. These specialized forms derive from nonfiction: the scholarly article, the idea in a journal, the field report, the critical essay, the book review. Such essay-like fictions are unlikely to engage deeply our senses or our hearts. But their attraction for the mind may be considerable.

The span of fiction's movement in this century has been narrower than that of painting, but the direction is the same: from depth to surface, from rondure to planes, from world to scheme, from observation to imagination, from story to theory, from society to individual, from emotion to mind. Literature as a whole has moved from contemplating cosmology—Dante—for the sake of God, to analyzing society—George Eliot—for the sake of man, to abstracting pattern itself—Nabokov—for the sake of art. At its purest, the new fiction parallels the scheme of, say, a Stevens lyric poem: in Nabokov's *Pale Fire*, fictional objects revolve about each other and only each other, and shed on each other and only each other a lovely and intellectual light.

In the contemporary modernist view, the work of art is above all a chunk in the hand. It is a self-lighted opacity, not a window and not a mirror. It is a painted sphere, not a crystal ball. The reader, then, must not wholly enter such a work of fiction; if he enters it emotionally, he will be lost, and miss the work's surface, where the framework of its meaning as art is spread. So the contemporary modernist fiction writer deliberately flattens the depth elements of his art. He replaces emotional strengths with intellectual ones. He makes his characters into interesting objects. He flattens narrative space-time by breaking it into bits; he flattens his story by fragmenting its parts and juxtaposing disparate elements on the page. He writes in sections; he interrupts himself by a hundred devices. In so doing, he keeps his readers fully conscious at his work's surface. Finally, he may wish to distance readers so thoroughly that he dispenses with character and narration altogether.

In *The Voices of Silence,* André Malraux likens storytelling in literature to representation in painting. Telling a story and painting a likeness of a face or a tree are sure-fire crowd-pleasers. (And for the idea of crowd-pleasing Malraux displays a fine Gallic contempt, in which he illogically does not include either storytelling or representation themselves.) Malraux is correct. A good story and a good representation have wide appeal. But his is a cheap shot. The more interesting comparison between storytelling in literature and representation in painting is this: that each was considered for centuries the irreducible nub of its art, and is no longer.

CHAPTER 3

The Fiction of Possibility

To round out a picture of contemporary modernist fiction, only a few more considerations remain. Art is modernist according to its handling, not according to its themes. Nevertheless, some themes are especially significant to recent contemporary modernist fiction. One of these is art itself.

Art About Art

Fiction has been redefining itself along theoretical lines. It has also been advancing its claim, throughout an increasing din from film, journalism, and advertising—not to mention the increasing din from the twentieth-century world at large—to be understood as art, as high holy art. Fiction has helped advance the successful claim of all the arts to be worth their candles. It has asserted its own purity, its disdain of mere commercialism, and its structural kinship with its poor and above-reproach cousin, lyric poetry. And in doing all this it has been increasingly interested in the subject of its own artfulness. So, of course, has painting. The enormously increased concern shown by both painting and fiction with their own art as their own subject matter reflects the overall self-consciousness of man in this century, I think; more specifically, it also reflects the quest for purity of practice which is born of this self-consciousness.

But painting is different. In contemporary painting, a work's surface and its subject matter—its form and content—may, and often do, entirely coincide: Frank Stella's "What you see is what you see." Words refer, and fiction's elements must always be bits of world; so fiction must ever quit its own surface and foray into the wide world in order to be about anything, even itself.

Language is weighted with referents. It is like a beam of light on Venus. There, on Venus, heavy atmospheric gravity bends light around the entire circumference of the planet, enabling a man, in theory, to see the back of his own head. Now, the object of every artist's vision is, in one sense, the back of his own head. But the writer, unlike the painter, sculptor, or composer, cannot form his idea of order directly in his materials; for as soon as he writes the least noun, the whole world starts pouring onto his page. So fiction, using language like a beam of Venusian light to see the back of its own head—to talk about its own art—makes a very wide tautological loop. It goes all around the world of language's referents before coming back to its own surface. It may, for instance, like

Pale Fire, create a world, or a grid for a world, which is an artful context for a set of meanings which in turn define art as the creation of worlds as artful contexts for meaning. Now, painting does such tricks directly, on a square of linen, with a line. There is a little paint, but there is no world, necessarily, between mind and hand. It is a game of inches. But fiction, happily, gets to go round via Zembla, or Yoknapatawpha County, or Dublin.

Fiction may be about art in a number of ways. All works of art are to some extent about art—but this way, as it is general, is meaningless. Fiction may talk about art by talking about art; this is common enough in many kinds of fiction. A novel's characters may be composers, poets, painters, or, especially, novelists. Gide's *The Counterfeiters*, published in 1926, was among the first of an undiminished spate of novels about a novelist who is trying to write a novel. Some of these end, predictably, when the hero seizes his or her pen and writes (on the very first try) the present novel's first words. Alternately, the protagonist's work-in-progress, described or even sampled in the text, serves as comment upon his own situation, or, more interestingly, acts as a gloss upon, or parody of, the living author's own future, unwritten novels (Nabokov, *The Real Life of Sebastian Knight*).

A work of art may be about art insofar as its referents never leave its own surface. This, as has been stressed, is a purely ideational state—it cannot occur in literature—but it can be approached. Gertrude Stein approached it. *Pale Fire* approaches it; its elements refer to each other in a brilliant snarl. If you were to cast the interconnected lumps of elements in *Pale Fire* into lines and geometric figures, into a chart of relationships, you would produce a Klee. To read *Pale Fire* you need English, you need the world evoked by the English, and you need, especially, a mental dictionary composed entirely of interdefined elements of *Pale Fire*. (The latter is true of any coherent text, of course, but it is especially true of those modernist texts which stress pattern over reference. Other clear cases might be Yeats's "Byzantium" or Stevens's "The Emperor of Ice Cream"—texts which baffle a reader until he locates or composes such a provisional dictionary, a set of terms defined internally by the text.) Much contemporary modernist fiction works in this way. The fragmented world becomes an art object contained on its own plane, a surface of refracting bits. The fiction transforms the world into a complex diagram. Whenever a work's own structure is, by intention, one of its own themes, another of its themes is art.

Related to the theme of art, but actually grounded in metaphysics, is the modernist attention to the relationship between a tale and its teller. When characters are telling the tale, and especially when they are telling it all cockeyed, the subject at hand may be not only the nature of art and the nature of narration, but also the nature of perception. Clearly, fictions which have a biased narrator, or many biased narrators, deal in part with perceptual bias as a theme. I am thinking here of works like Nabokov's *Despair* with its sole viewpoint or Durrell's *Alexandria Quartet* with its many. But perceptual bias is not limited to cranky characters. It is every artist's stock-in-trade. It is every perceiver's stock-in-trade. And, as the thinking artist knows full well, everyone is cockeyed. Since everyone is cockeyed, what can anyone perceive truly? What can we know, or what can we say of the world? Gradually, then, the question of the relationship between tale, teller, and world fades into the question of the relationship between any perceiver and any object. And this matter is a frequent theme—nay, obsession—in contemporary modernist fiction.

The Problem of Knowing the World

Any penetrating interest in anything ultimately leads to what used to be called epistemology. If you undertake the least mental task—if you so much as try to classify a fern—you end up agog in the lap of Kant. For in order to know anything for certain, we must first examine the mind's own way of knowing. And how on earth do we propose to do that?

This is a live issue in this country. John Dewey pointed out, quite intelligently, that philosophy progresses not by solving problems but by abandoning them. It simply loses interest. The question of "epistemology" is one which thinkers of this century have not yet abandoned. On the contrary, everybody seems to be working on it. So much interesting work is being done outside the field of philosophy proper, and outside philosophy's terms, that it seems appropriate now to replace the term epistemology with a new term—such as cognition—to refer to this new wealth of related topics.

Examining the structures of human thought and perception are recent thinkers like Paul Weiss and Ludwig Von Bertalanffy in systems theory, Gregory Bateson in information theory, Roman Jakobson and Thomas Sebeok in semiotics, Noam Chomsky in linguistics, John Eccles and Wilder Penfield in brain physiology, Claude Lévi-Strauss and Mary Douglas in anthropology, Ernst Gombrich in art criticism, and Jerome Bruner and Jean Piaget in psychology. They seek to understand the processes by which the mind imposes order. They seek to clarify the relationship between perceiving and thinking, between inventing and knowing. Microphysicists are interested in these matters too. Science as a whole, like philosophy, wants to proceed from a firm base. Interestingly, the human effort to locate that base, to set knowledge firmly upon the plinth of perception, seems repeatedly to result in everybody's sinking at once. At any rate, I think the interest in cognition derives ultimately from a genuine interest in the world for its own sake. And I imagine that Western thought intended simply to get this little business out of the way, so it could proceed with its task of tracing quarks or analyzing texts; but no one has been able to get it out of the way. Instead, it just gets more interesting in its own right.

From the time of Greek science till now, Western culture has usually had a lively, unselfish, and intellectual interest in the phenomenal world for its own sake. Historians of culture think that this interest sprang originally from meeting cultures. In the port towns at the peripheries of major civilizations, people of varying cultures and religions met. They soon asked themselves (according to this theory) what could be true if men disagreed, and if one world view was apparently as workable as another. This innocent inquiry—an inquiry it would have been impossible to make from the middle of China, the middle of Egypt, or the middle of Mexico—led straight to the moon. It is, then, a very good question, and we have not stopped asking it. What is absolutely true? What can we know for certain? What is really here?

In fact, we are asking these questions now with fresh

urgency. Of course, we in the West agree now that there is more than one way to skin a cat, or raise a baby, or help pain, or live. And no one is losing much sleep now over the idea that our tribal gods are not absolute. But we *are* having a slow century of it, digesting the information that our yardsticks are not absolute, our mathematics is not absolute.

Science, that product of skepticism born of cultural diversity, is meant to deal in certainties, in data which anyone anywhere could verify. And for the most part it has. Our self-referential mathematics and wiggly yardsticks got us to the moon. I think science works the way a tightrope walker works: by not looking at its feet. As soon as it looks at its feet, it realizes it is operating in midair. At any rate, the sciences are wondering again, as the earliest skeptics did, what could be a firm basis for knowledge. People in many of the sciences are looking at their feet. First Einstein, then Heisenberg, then Gödel, made a shambles of our hope (a hope which Kant shared) for a purely natural science which actually and certainly connects at base with things as they are. What can we know for certain when our position in space is limited, our velocity may vary, our instruments contract as they accelerate, our observations of particles on the microlevel botch our own chance of precise data, and not only are our own senses severely limited, but many of the impulses they transmit are edited out before they ever reach the brain?

Even if we could depend on our senses, could we trust our brains? Even if science could depend on its own data, would it not still have to paw through its own language and cultural assumptions, its *a priori* categories, wishes, and so forth, to approach things as they are? To what, in fact, could the phrase "things as they are" meaningfully refer apart from all our discredited perceptions, to which everything is so inextricably stuck? Physicists have been saying for sixty years that (according to the Principle of Indeterminacy) they cannot study nature, but only their own perception of nature: "method and object can no longer be separated" (Heisenberg). Sir Arthur Stanley Eddington, British Astronomer Royal, said in 1927: "The physical world is entirely abstract and without 'actuality' apart from its linkage to consciousness." It is one thing when Berkeley says this; when a twentieth-century astronomer says this, it is a bit of another thing. Similarly (and this is more familiar), Eddington's successor Sir James Jeans wrote, summarizing a series of findings in physics: "The world begins to look more like a great thought than a great machine." The world could be, then, in Eddington's phrase, "mind-stuff." And even the mind, anthropologists keep telling us, is not so much a cognitive instrument as a cultural artifact. The mind is itself an art object. It is a Mondrian canvas onto whose homemade grids it fits its own preselected products. Our knowledge is contextual and only contextual. Ordering and invention coincide: we call their collaboration "knowledge." The mind is a blue guitar on which we improvise the song of the world.

The Fiction of Possibility

Where does fiction fit into all this? For one thing, the interdisciplinary treatment of these issues is in a state so lively it is scarcely distinguishable from outright disarray, and fiction writers, like everyone else, are drawn to messes. Fiction writers are as interested in their century's intellectual issues as any other thinkers. Fiction, like painting, intrinsically deals with the nature of perception. And fiction intrinsically deals with the world. So that finally fiction, if it has anything at all to do with the world as its subject matter, will begin to ask, What world?

Early in *Swann's Way*, Marcel recalls:

> When I saw any external object, my consciousness that I was seeing it would remain between me and it, enclosing it in a slender, incorporeal outline which prevented me from ever coming directly in contact with the material form.

This is one way that fiction may pose the problem of cognition. How may we come "directly in contact" with "any external object"? Some writers approach it by wresting the object from the grip of its ordinary contexts, so that we see it as it were for the first time. Surrealism racks its brains to dislocate ordinary expectations; it wrenches objects from their ordinary mental settings until at last (it hopes) it unhinges the mind itself.

Writers may also approach fresh vision by restraining their painterly impulses and using language as a cognitive tool. That is, fresh vision is an unstated goal but a guiding one, I think, in fiction written in that very plain, exact, unemotional prose which contemporary writers of both traditional and modernist fiction use to describe the world of objects. Writers like Henry Green and Wright Morris on one hand, and Alain Robbe-Grillet on the other, write as if the world were indeed here and fiction owed it the responsibility of a careful and unbiased attention. Robbe-Grillet wishes the writer to limit his efforts to describing the surfaces of things and measuring the distances between them. On this effort he comments (my emphasis): *"This comes down to establishing that things are here."* Establishing that things are here is, so far as I know, a new goal for art. And establishing that things are here is no mean feat: it is an effort that kept Kant and Wittgenstein quite occupied.

Some fiction deals with matters of cognition more directly. Stanislaw Lem's *The Cyberiad*, which describes the plottings of two rival computer makers, concerns the nature of knowing. Also concerned implicitly with the nature of knowing are detective and mystery stories, and, explicitly, contemporary modernist fictions using detective or mystery conventions, like Robbe-Grillet's *The Voyeur* and Borges's "Death and the Compass." Other fiction, of which the *Alexandria Quartet* is the clearest type, deliberately treats the "relativity" of all knowledge by presenting a series of narratives which contradict. Still other fiction mimics the unknowableness of the world by being itself unknowable. It works—if it works—by eliciting confusion. If you track down some of the allusions and puzzles in *Pale Fire*, what you get amounts to a Bronx cheer.

In many works, the world is the arena of possibilities. Anything may happen. This "anything" is fiction's new subject. Traditional writers labor to make their "what-ifs" seem plausible. But contemporary modernists flaunt the speculative nature of their fiction. What if, they say, and what if what else? Italo Calvino's *Invisible Cities* is a wonderful case in point. In this book, Marco Polo reports to Kublai Khan on the many cities he has discovered by exploring the khan's realm. Each description of a city is formal and titled (with a woman's name); each occupies about a page. There is the city hung from high nets suspended over a plain; there is the city whose inhabitants stretch string all over town to delineate their every relationship, until the strings make a web in which no one can move; there is the city whose carnival stays put year after year while its banks, docks, and municipal buildings are loaded onto trucks and taken on tour. After every few descriptions of cities, Marco Polo and the khan discuss the reports; many of their discussions hinge on the question of whether Marco Polo is making everything up. But what, in the realm of imagination, could be the difference between invention and discovery? And is not all the world the realm of Kublai Khan, the realm of imagination?

If to the artist, and to the mind, each of the world's bits is a mental object for contemplation or manipulation, then those bits may be actual or fancied; it does not matter which. They may derive indifferently from newspaper accounts or dreams. And since mental objects and imaginary objects have equal status, the man of imagination is the creator of the world.

These ideas, I say, underly some of the best contemporary modernist fiction. They dominate the work of Borges, Nabokov, and Calvino; we find them also in many other writers, like Barth, Coover, Cortázar, Gilbert Sorrentino, Guy Davenport, Flann O'Brien, and almost any other contemporary modernist we can name. Some works stress the role of mind in actively shaping reality, as Borges's "Tlön, Uqbar, Orbis Tertius" does. In this story, the inhabitants of the planet Tlön—which was itself invented and set in motion by a series of thinkers—may through their expectations call objects into being. If a man is looking for a lost pencil, he may find, not the original pencil, but a secondary object, "more in keeping with his expectation." "These secondary objects are called *hrönir* and, even though awkward in form, are a little larger than the originals." The people may also bring another class of objects into being; an *ur* is "an object brought into being by hope." (The subject at hand in this frankly philosophical story is the nature of Berkeley's idealism.)

Other works, like Nabokov's *The Real Life of Sebastian Knight*, stress the role of the conscious artist as imagination's lord. If inventing is knowing, and if meaning is contextual, then the artist is the supreme knower and the artificer of meaning. Still other works, like Lem's *A Perfect Vacuum* and Borges's "Pierre Menard, Author of Don Quixote," which are modeled on the interpretation of texts, stress the equal status of all mental objects. Imaginary or third-hand texts, or accounts of texts, have not only the same ontological status as canonical texts, but also the same status and capacity for meaning as actual events. And actual events may be interpreted as if they were texts. Everything on earth or in imagination is a conjunction of mental objects; it is an art object which may be interpreted critically.

The world, happily, still exists, and contemporary modernist fiction still interprets it. One interpretation to which these same writers are prone is a reading of the world in the light of its multiple material combinations. We scarcely require imagination to produce a wealth of possible conjunctions; the actual world is doing very well on its own. In these works, such as Calvino's *Cosmicomics,* Cortázar's *Hopscotch,* or Borges's "The Aleph," the artist's generative role is again secret, and the dizzying multiplicity of the world itself is the subject. I think that the new sense of stellar and geologic time we have in this century, and the reiterated tale of how chemicals evolve, and how new species arise from random combinations in multiple circumstances over unimaginably long reaches of time, must surely contribute to this contemporary fiction of possibility. The work of Calvino and Borges, at least, is visibly stricken with a sense of a finite material world so long and wide it becomes a material metaphor for infinity. Beckett and Borges treat these matters soberly; other writers, like Barth, Cortázar, and Coover, seem to grow giddy at the thought, as if creating were not the deliberate work Genesis made it out to be, but instead God's spendthrift and neverending jubilee.

Writers and artists of this century may well ascribe to their work a new and real importance. If art is the creation of contexts, *and so is everything else,* how false or trivial can art be? Was not the Linnaean system of classification a poem among poems, a provisional coherence selected out of chaos? It has always been possible for artists of every kind of sniff at science and claim for art special, transcendent, and priestly powers. Now it is possible for artists to have and eat that particular cake by adding that, after all, science is in one (rather attenuated) sense "mere" art; art is all there is. I am not saying that writers or painters have made such a claim—but it is there to be made.

This, then, is contemporary modernist fiction. Its themes are its own artfulness and pattern, and the nature of a world newly elusive and material, and a mind newly aware of its limits, and an imagination newly loosed. Technically as well as thematically it has taught us to admire the surfacing of structure and device. It prizes subtlety more than drama, concision more than expansion, parody more than earnestness, artfulness more than verisimilitude, intellection more than entertainment. It concerns itself less with social classes than with individuals, and, structurally, less with individual growth than with pattern of idea. It is not a statement but an artifact. Instead of social, moral, or religious piety or certainty, and emotional depth, it offers humor, irony, intellectual complexity, technical beauty, and a catalogue of the forms of unknowing.

I should say in conclusion, before we leave modernism altogether, that the modernist direction in all the arts is a movement from what might be called the organic to the inorganic. Traditional painting, sculpture, fiction, poetry, drama, and, lesserly, music since the Renaissance deal in organic forms in which materials as it were flow from each other. The work moves and grows across time with an imitated living energy; cause precedes effect, "leaf subsides to leaf," chord yields to chord tonally, and the leg bone attaches to the . . . hip bone. Modernist forms, on the other hand, are inorganic, as a triangle is inorganic, as a model of the atom is fixed and unmoving. (At least half of painting's major movements in this century have promoted inorganic structures: Constructivism, Suprematism, some Futurism, Orphism, Analytic Cubism, *Abstraction-Créationism*, Geometric Abstraction, and color field painting.) We can watch Mondrian transform an apple tree, and a drawing of an apple tree, into a grid of inorganic forms. Cézanne found the cylinder in the thigh. Yeats enjoined his actors not to move; Beckett props prevented their moving. Schönberg purged chromatic movement of tonal content and won through to a scaffolding of pure form. And contemporary modernist fiction disassembles human life in time. It dissects the living, articulated joints and arranges the bright bones on the ground.

Where Is the Mainstream?

The description I have given of contemporary modernist fiction is piecework. It extracts, collates, and examines as a unit such diversities as say, the characterizations of Borges or Pynchon, the narrative collages and surrealisms of Burroughs or Barthelme, the ironies of Beckett or Disch, the aesthetics or metaphysics of Barth or Calvino, and the cryptographic surfaces and reflexive structures of Nabokov. In fact, no single writer matches in all his work every aspect of this theoretical description. My coarse distinctions between two kinds of fiction are useful heuristically, but they give a damaging impression of clear boundaries and a misleading impression of two armed camps.

I have not yet stressed that most contemporary writers write largely traditional fiction. Many excellent writers, like Graham Greene, John Updike, Joyce Cary, Anthony Powell, and many others, are writing a fiction whose virtues are largely those of realist or naturalist fiction. After all, if we posit traditional fiction at one extreme of a spectrum and contemporary modernism at the other extreme, we see that not only do most living writers of serious fiction belong near the spectrum's center, but so also do the historical Modernists themselves. The Modernists—Kafka, Proust, Faulkner, Joyce—were interested in society, deepened time, verisimilitude, complex character, and authorial austerity. They were a sincere lot. They wrote big books. Contemporary modernists alter their aims by isolating them.

In fact, on a very gloomy day one could say this: that contemporary modernism accurately puts its finger upon, and claims, every quality of Modernist fiction that is not essential. It throws out the baby and proclaims the bath.

Joyce wrote parodies and made puns and allusions on his way to elaborating a full and deep fictional world called Dublin. Now people write little parodies full of puns and allusions. Kafka wrote fiction rooted in profound cultural criticism and in metaphysical and theological longing; along the way he had a character turn into a cockroach. Some contemporary writing has jettisoned the rest and kept the cockroach for a laugh. Joyce and Woolf bade their characters think on the page to deepen the characters, not to flatten the world solipsistically. Proust and Faulkner fiddled with time to create an artful simulacrum of our experience of time and also our knowledge of the world; now some contemporary writing may fiddle with time to keep us awake, the way television commercials splice scenes to keep us awake, or they may fiddle with time to distract us from the absence of narration, or even just to fiddle. The wit that was perhaps incidental in Joyce has become an end in itself. In short, Modernist writers expanded fictional techniques in the service of traditional ends—one could say on this putative very gloomy day—and those ends have been lost. On the other hand, of course, great contemporary modernists bend those techniques to new interesting, and valuable, ends, as I think I have shown.

The Modernists themselves, I say, begin to look semi-traditional in the light of contemporary practice. It is not unreasonable to place *The Castle, Ulysses,* or *Light in August* near the center of a spectrum on which we place *Great Expectations* or *The Charterhouse of Parma* at one end and *Pale Fire, Hopscotch,* and *Ficciones* at the other. And given these extremes, it is easy to see that most living writers also belong somewhere in the middle. Most often these writers, like the Modernists themselves, bend sophisticated techniques toward traditional ends. Here are the many writers of serious fiction—including the majority of writers in the Americas, Britain, and Europe whose work is widely known, as well as many other excellent and great writers as yet uncelebrated—who are writing novels and stories of depth and power, novels and stories which penetrate the world and order it, which engage us intellectually and move us emotionally, which render complex characters in depth, treat moral concerns and issues, make free use of modernist techniques, and astonish us by the fullness and coherence of their artifice. This is still, if only by volume, the mainstream.

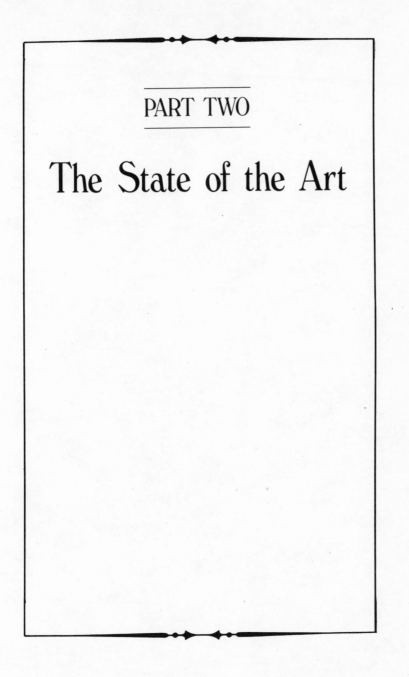

PART TWO

The State of the Art

CHAPTER 4

Revolution, No

I have asserted, but not yet defended, the notion that fiction cannot shed the world because its materials are necessarily bits of world. The writer's materials, common sense says, are various characters, places, actions, ideas, and actual or mental objects. The writer's materials are real or imagined phenomena.

One could say, however, that the writer's materials are words and the other paraphernalia of language. After all, a writer does not sit at his desk pushing little people and landscapes around. He manipulates words like so many dabs of paint. And who is to say that the words correspond to anything? I want to treat this idea with some respect before I discard it.

Language scarcely accounts for things, or for the flux

and mystery of experience. If it did, Romantic poets could go about their task with the aplomb of bricklayers. We know that language itself is a selection and abstraction from unknowable flux; the world shades into gradations too fine for speech. A Jerome Bruner study shows that human eyes can distinguish among approximately twenty thousand colors. Yet English, a language rich in color terms, names only a few score of them; some languages name only three or four. Language, like other cognitive structures, is useful for some tasks and worthless for others. I cannot tell you, because I do not know, what my language prevents my knowing. Language is itself like a work of art; it selects, abstracts, exaggerates, and orders. How then could we say that language encloses and signifies phenomena, when language is a fabricated grid someone stuck in a river? Or how can we even say that language communicates by agreed-upon convention, when people personalize symbols so readily, so that a word which means life to me may mean death to you, and we cannot agree?

We must grant, then, that words for things miss their marks, or at least, as I see it, obscure things here and there around the edges. And we grant, sighing, that we see through a cultural-linguistic glass darkly, and cannot tell snow from snow. Nevertheless, the plain fact is that language does serve literary purposes adequately.

To be quite precise, we must say that a writer's language does not signify things as they are—because none of us knows things as they are; instead, a writer's language does an airtight job of signifying his *perceptions* of things as they are. The term "salty" may hopelessly confine my perceptions—my sensations—when I taste saltiness, so that I miss a dozen accompanying sensations and taste only saltiness. You suffer the same loss. Well, then, the term "salty," which so dictates how we perceive, at least expresses *what* we perceive, very well, and also communicates it to those afflicted with the same language. Language need not know the world perfectly in order to communicate perceptions adequately.

Language actually signifies things transparently, in a way that paint must labor to do. The word "apple" signifies appledom (or our perception of appledom) to all of us, and we will politely suspend our private meanings for the word in order to hear each other out. If I write "apple," I can make you think of a mental apple roughly analogous to the one I have in mind. But I am hard put to make you think of a certain arrangement of alphabet letters or phonemes. The word itself all but vanishes, like Vermeer's paint.

The writer, then, composes with mental objects, actual or imagined; he composes with what Poe called "the things and thoughts of time." Dickens drew his materials in *Bleak House* from the breadth of London society and from contemporary British legal usage; it were madness, or quibbling, to say he drew them from a dictionary.

The upshot of all this, as I have suggested, is that fiction cannot escape the world as its necessary subject matter. Hence it cannot break with its own traditions, or throw its criticism into crisis, or lose its audience, or move its action entirely to its own surface. Whether a writer writes "grapefruit," or "God," or "freedom," his indispensable subject matter is the world beyond the page. Even when Joyce writes (to cite a familiar example), "Nobirdy aviar soar anywing to eagle it!" his passage does not eliminate referents; it multiplies them.

One notable effort to alter the subject matter of fiction—Gertrude Stein's—was an effort to alter the subject matter of language. Her aim (like that of Juan Gris, the similarity of whose work to hers she acknowledged) was "exactitude." "A star glide," she wrote, "a frantic sullenness, a single financial grass greediness." "Toasted susie," she wrote, "is my ice cream." Stein's work, and *Finnegans Wake*, come close to vaporizing the world and making of language a genuine stuff. Often Stein's work achieves the unity of a single plane which glitters with a thousand refractions where the words, bound together at the surface, still tilt in every direction toward their referents in the world.

Stein's writing brought forth no revolution; neither did *Finnegans Wake*. Literature co-opted them; they joined the canon with scarcely a ripple, and inspired few successors. What Stein did, and what Joyce did in *Finnegans Wake*, was playfully to misread the nature of fiction. Fiction could have moved its arena to its own material surface, to virtually nobody's interest, if fiction's materials had really been words, and if writers had succeeded in detaching the words from their referents. But fiction's materials are bits of world. Fiction's subject matter can indeed move very far in the direction of its own surfaces; but those surfaces are not language surfaces but referential narrative objects. It turned out, then, that *Ulysses*, with its broken narrative surface, indicated a more fruitful and honest modernist direction for fiction.

The movement toward the modernist in fiction is one of emphasis. It is a shifting stance, not an outright leap. Just as there has been no sudden shift to abstraction in fiction, because the nature of fiction's materials prevents it, so also there has been no sudden shift to contemporary modernism in fiction, because the nature of everything else prevents it. Before I get to this interesting "everything else," let me make this point. Mere change is not revolution. The contemporary modernists are here, all right, but they did not slay the old guard in their beds. Instead, the old guard liked their looks, invited them in, and exchanged a few tricks with them after dinner.

This assertion is controversial. Robert Scholes, in his excellent *Fabulation and Metafiction*, argues at one point that contemporary modernism has replaced traditional fiction. Those who write the old fiction constitute "a small school of neo-naturalists" who write "frantically, headless chickens unaware of the decapitating axe." This is perfectly true, as far as it goes; a purely naturalist fiction today is an absurd relic, like a horseshoe crab, especially if it is, in Scholes's terms, "unaware."

But who is unaware? Only undergraduates who try to write without having read. Surely critics are not in the business of berating the ignorant. Woody Allen uses modernist techniques freely; so do television commercials. You can no more avoid either the techniques or the aesthetic they express than you can avoid the Mondrian look at Penney's. If someone out there is writing a purely naturalist fiction, using only nineteenth-century techniques, he is not so much a chicken with his head cut off as a dead horse.

The notion of "schools" does not work because neither set of writers constitutes a school. If we admit, as Scholes does, Lawrence Durrell, Bernard Malamud, John Fowles, and Iris Murdoch to the new school—and this is only reasonable—then what have we proved? That the new school has wielded its axe in triumph, or that almost all decent living novelists are capable of using techniques developed sixty years ago?

The techniques have been around for centuries, even, if you want to go back to Sterne, and writers are perfectly aware of them. If someone like Saul Bellow does not want to use them, he is not, I think, unaware, or making a last stand; rather, he would prefer not to.* Fiction writers are aiming at eternity, I do believe, and not at each other, and not at the power to determine fiction's direction. And in the house of eternity there are many mansions.

Fiction has expanded its borders. Nothing has killed or replaced anything. The old co-opted the new. Everywhere, categories overlap. Even if we name names we get into trouble. There is no such animal as a thoroughgoing, cradle-to-grave contemporary modernist outside France. Pynchon and others describe society; Nabokov, Beckett, and Barth round character; many contemporary modernists imitate the unbroken flow of time; *Ada* brims with emotion; some surrealist work is a bit skimpy on idea; and Borges of late seems to quit the library and hunker instead at a neolithic campfire, bringing fiction full circle to its putative beginnings. As Scholes is pointing out, almost all contemporary writers use the new techniques. Where would Frederick Buechner belong? Larry Woiwode? Evan S. Connell, Jr.? Lessing? Garrett's *Death of the Fox?* Updike's *The Centaur?* Grass's *The Tin Drum?*

Of course, it is false logic to maintain that where boundaries are blurred, no distinctions exist. Just because no one can specify at which smudge a clean wall becomes a dirty wall, that does not mean there is no difference between a clean wall and a dirty wall. There are abun-

*There are no opposing camps; there is no struggle. Each writer is a one-man camp, unallied and unarmed, a lone bivouac under heaven.

dant differences between naturalist fiction and contemporary modernist fiction. But there are simply too many writers and works of fiction which do excellent things in both categories for anyone to talk about revolution or even opposing schools.

If we grant that fiction has changed gradually, we still get to ask why it has not changed wholly. Why is anyone still writing "neo-naturalist" fiction? Why, since everyone can see fiction's direction as plain as day, does anyone fail to follow the pointing finger? How could anyone prefer not to?

I have said that the writer is aiming at eternity—at perfecting his art. The writer of traditional fiction may see fiction as a form both solid and open, one which permits him to assault perfection from any intelligent stance without fear of ridicule. (No one is laughing at Saul Bellow, after all.) On the other hand, such a writer may have motives personal as well as theoretical. He may like the world of things. Or he may wish to keep a roof over his head.

Fiction, insofar as it is traditional, has a large and paying audience whose tastes serve to keep it traditional. Shall we deny this, or merely deplore it? As Emerson said of the fall of man, "It is very unhappy, but too late to be helped." But, one could find in the fall of man, or even in the mass audience for fiction, a certain grim felicity. The next chapter will detail some colorful and low-down reasons why contemporary modernist fiction does not wholly dominate the field.

CHAPTER 5

Marketplace and Bazaar

Oddly, almost everyone who can read feels qualified to discuss works of fiction, and even to discuss their merits and demerits in print. You could work yourself into a genuine froth over this: everyone who reads fiction seems to feel qualified to review it. One might as well let children, who eat, judge restaurants. Some book reviewers have no training in literature whatever. Now, no one would collar a man in the street to review a showing of a contemporary painter's work. The man in the street would be decent enough to beg off. So why do people with no special training in literature discuss so unabashedly their tastes in fiction?

The preceding paragraph was a hoax. I want you to feel, as I mostly do, that although its argument has a few merits in the abstract, it is essentially elitist, curmudgeon-ly, and morally wrong. Why? We would swallow the same argument about painting or music without demur. Clearly, our assumptions about fiction are different.

In the simple answer to this exaggerated question lies one of fiction's great strengths. It is of course that fiction, as a field, is not entirely the prerogative of specialists. And the fact that fiction is not the prerogative of special-ists militates in favor of its traditional virtues simply be-cause nonspecialists prefer depth to abstract surface. Spe-cialists are interested in form; nonspecialists like lots of realized content.

This little social phenomenon is more a symptom than a cause; but it is an interesting one. How many educated Westerners feel free to comment, especially negatively, outside their fields? Who apart from specialists will say of a Di Suvero sculpture, "It doesn't work," or of a Alvin Lucier composition, "It's no good"? Yet who hesitates to rate contemporary novels? This symptom reveals the as-sumption that fiction, even when it is literature, should answer to its audience by pleasing it. The notion is still abroad, even, that pleasing an audience is precisely what the fiction writer had in mind. Given these assumptions, any member of the audience—any reader—naturally prizes his own reactions and considers them useful and pertinent. The extreme of this position is Philistinism, which permits a reader to fume and rage, disbelieving, at those contemporary modernist works which do not en-gage him. The Philistine does not fume and rage on the grounds that the writers' aims are uncongenial, but on the unquestioned assumption that writers *intend* to be congenial first and foremost, that writers' aims are changeless, that everyone is trying to be Charles Dickens.

Of course, by these lights the works fail miserably, and the reader is aghast that living writers could so lack talent to please, and suspects a hoax.

But Philistinism in the raw is not our present concern; and although all this is decidedly unnerving, it is by and large a healthy state. That fiction is not yet the exclusive province of specialists, that those who make it their business to understand it are not quite yet priests, that most of it requires of its audience no initiate status—these things distinguish fiction from most of the best contemporary poetry, music, painting, and sculpture. Fiction has a wide audience. The audience that a serious short story writer or novelist may address is literate and perhaps educated; but it is not necessarily educated in the formal issues of literature per se. All sorts of people read good fiction. All sorts of people may not read Henry Green or Julio Cortázar or Italo Calvino, or even Henry James, Bruno Schulz, or Samuel Beckett, but all sorts of people do read Faulkner, García Márquez, Nabokov, and Grass, say, and the contemporary picaresque novelists. By contrast, the other contemporary arts are marvelously down to essences. They have rid themselves of all impure elements, including an audience.

Fiction keeps its audience by retaining the world as its subject matter. People like the world. Many people actually prefer it to art and spend their days by choice in the thick of it. The world's abounding objects, its rampant variety of people, its exuberant, destructive, and unguessable changes, and the splendid interest of its multiple conjunctions, appeal, attract, and engage more than ideas do, and more than beauty bare. When the arts abandon the world as their subject matter, people abandon the arts. And when wide audiences abandon the arts, the arts are free to pursue whatever theories led them to abandon the world in the first place. They are as free as wandering albatrosses or stamp collectors or technical rock climbers; no one is looking.

I would be the last to argue that fiction's wide audience keeps it responsible. Anyone could far more easily argue that it keeps it mediocre and stunted. This latter position is as familiar and self-evident as it is valid. God only knows what works of art will not see print in this generation, or ever, in the name of that wide audience whose wide neck one so often wishes to wring. Fiction's wide audience does not keep it responsible; it merely inhibits its development away from the traditional.

Contemporary modernist works, which concern themselves as much with the solution of their own formal and intellectual problems as with the peopled world, have no very wide audience save for a few isolated works, like *Lolita* and *Giles Goat-Boy*—which in fact treat of the great world more than their sibling works *The Gift*, say, or *Chimera*. The taste of fiction's wide audience inadvertently preserves fiction in its historical context and keeps fiction's aesthetic impure. These things in turn enable fiction to maintain a breadth of practice, a material density, and a richness of inventive possibility.

All this works only because the wishes of fiction's audience carry weight. So long as fiction is mass marketed, the taste of the "mass" is a *force majeure*. By contrast, the audience preference for representative easel painting is as irrelevant as wind. The audience is no longer attached to the mechanism. The powerful force which drew such enormous crowds—hardly Philistines or mere nostalgics—to the Museum of Modern Art and the Metropolitan Museum for their Degas, Cézanne, and Monet exhibits is virtually lost, unharnessed to the mechanism of contemporary practice, which whirs, pops, and whistles along untouched in its several corners.

Its wide and influential audience is only one of many factors which keep fiction traditional. Each of these factors, as it muddies the purity of fiction as art, also enhances its popularity. Similarly, everything which encourages fiction's audience also, and incidentally, discourages developments in contemporary modernism.

A case in point is the blurring of fictional genres. Fictional genres blur in a way that plastic art genres have not done since Cellini and Ghiberti turned out hope chests and salt cellars. We do not find Sol LeWitt painting on velvet, nor Rauschenberg trying his hand at motel art. Yet we do find writers of real stature writing literature in any category: spy and detective novels (Chandler), murder mysteries (Robbe-Grillet), gothic romances (Murdoch), fantasies (Calvino), fairy tales (Barth), and science fiction (Disch). We cannot eliminate any genre or any materials across the board, saying, This cannot be art. (Similarly, the large audiences for these sorts of fiction are broad-minded and generous; they do not, I think, discriminate against literature, saying of a Graham Greene spy novel, This cannot be good.)

Publishers encourage this healthy confusion, seeking readers where they can. They fertilize these fields heavily, and reap the harvest. The advertising and jacket copy of books make little or no distinctions between junk fiction and works of art, and in fact may cloud the issue. The issue is certainly clouded anyway. It is clouded even in the minds of critics, even in the minds of writers: who among serious literary novelists or short story writers dearly wishes not to be widely read? And conversely, what junk novelist, no matter how calculating, no matter how languidly he taped his latest blockbuster from the deck of no matter how large a boat, will dismiss any suggestion that his novels may, in fact, in part, in significance, or in skill, in the long run be considered literature?

The journals which print reviews also seem at times to dwell in a marketing wonderland of undifferentiated objects called "books." If the new Updike novel is good and the new Junker is good, reviews saying so are apt to appear on facing pages. Rarely does one find a printed distinction drawn between real literature and mere entertainment. It is as though distinctions, per se, might be thought illiberal. Since most serious contemporary fiction falls somewhere between realism and contemporary modernism, and since good literature is usually entertaining, most new novels please in many ways. Both reviewers and the journals which print reviews would be hard put to define all these overlapping categories.

No one, in fact, is losing sleep over these things anyway—over the blurring of genres in fiction and the blurred distinctions between literature and non-literature—although they interest me enormously. Is *Appointment in Samarra* literature? *Sweet Thursday?* *The Bridge of San Luis Rey?* Is *On the Road* literature? If it is, was it when it was published?

Of course, literary fashion, which may determine which contemporary works are considered canonical, is a whimsical thing, determined by nobody in particular, and stressing authors as dead personalities. As I go to press, for instance, Steinbeck's stock seems to be very low, and presumably that of his novels as well, on the wondrous grounds that he was not always a nice guy, and even on the grounds that as a philosopher (!) he was not entirely original, but instead openly acknowledged that his friend Ed Ricketts influenced his thinking. Similarly, Flannery O'Connor's stock seems to be high at the moment, and perhaps even, by extension, that of her cryptic, Catholic stories, on the grounds that her posthumous letters show that she was witty and knew her place. The concepts of canon and literature do not coincide. Canon is an historical category which includes failed works of literature like Shakespeare's worst play and *Uncle Tom's Cabin*. Contemporary works of highest-quality literature, like Fred Chappell's novels say, or Doris Betts's stories, are not yet canonical; they must wait until time, or the cult of personality, catches up with them.

Among works of nonfiction, which are literature and which are not? Surely there is a distinction between such works as *A River Runs Through It*, *Green Hills of Africa*, and *Wind, Sand and Stars* and other nonfiction, from field guides to cookbooks. But where are the boundaries? Is *In Patagonia* literature? People seem to think so, apparently because it is very well written, sentence by sentence, and nothing happens in it. Precisely where does journalism or memoir become literature? Surely Gorky's *My Childhood* and Nabokov's *Speak, Memory* are literature, because Gorky and Nabokov are canonical. But what of John Cowper Powys's *Autobiography*? This is a strong, vivid, and eccentric artifice whose author is not quite canonical.

I have never read a story better than *Endurance*, Alfred Lansing's account of the Shackleton expedition to Antarctica; but no one considers it literature. If Mailer had written it, might we not read the same text as a parable of something or other? The matter of context here is interesting. When Capote called *In Cold Blood* literature, he made it more likely to be read as literature than is, say, *Hiroshima*, whose author kept mum.

Mailer's *The Executioner's Song* is the new case in point. Mailer's calling this documentary account of the life and death of convict Gary Gilmore a novel seems to say, This text is meaningful, it is a work of art. The cultural assumption is that the novel is the proper home of significance and that nonfiction is mere journalism. This is interesting because it means that in two centuries our assumptions have been reversed. Formerly the novel was junk entertainment; if you wanted to write significant literature—if you wanted to do art or make an object from ideas—you wrote nonfiction. We now think of nonfiction as sincere and artless. According to Wesleyan historian Henry Abelove, this changed assumption makes it impossible for modern historians to understand seventeenth- and eighteenth-century texts so long as they assume that people have always written essays in order to proffer ideas in which they sincerely believed. In fact, writers then were more apt to write essays for the same reason that Wallace Stevens wrote poems. Now we have come half circle. Now the novel is seen as the literary form, the art form. This is actually great news, for which we have to thank generations of serious novelists and also the defenders of the novel at the much-publicized 1933 *Ulysses* controversy. Less great are its implications for nonfiction.

Mailer gets it both ways. Nonfiction is more popular than fiction; but no one is in danger of mistaking *The Executioner's Song* for invention. What if another novelist, say a housewife in Illinois, contrived a novel about a fictional murderer who was executed to national fanfare?

What if this fabrication matched Gary Gilmore's actual life? What if it matched Mailer's text? Would the meaning be the same? Would anyone give a blessed fig? If you want to analyze society, people will listen to your data, but not your parables. Diane Johnson, reviewing *The Executioner's Song* for the *New York Review of Books*, wrote: "It is finally the fact that all this really happened that moves us most."

Similar juggling of context surrounds Melville's *The Encantadas*. This wonderful essay, a wholly factual account of the Galapagos Islands, is always considered fiction—for no reason which I can learn. Is it because Melville usually wrote fiction? Is it because it is narrative? Is it because the characters are colorful? Is it because it is *good?* Or is it because much of it is hearsay?

What if Darwin had written *The Encantadas* word for word? Ruth Benedict wrote the classic anthropological study of Japan, *The Chrysanthemum and the Sword*, without ever having seen Japan; no one considers it fiction. What if Borges had written *The Chrysanthemum and the Sword?* Borges's intention, his times, the sophistication of his audience, and especially the context of his other works, would create a wholly new set of meanings for the work—the Pierre Menard complex.

The context into which a work is received actually affects its meaning (despite a century's valuable efforts from formalist critics), and this context can be manipulated. What is the context into which publishers launch a work of fiction by an unknown author? It could be, theoretically, that a writer's intentions cannot affect his work's contents so much as his publisher's intentions can. Could a publisher's tampering with a work actually alter its meaning? I think so. Imagine a publisher's whimsically aiming a new detective novel—whose author intended it to sell like hotcakes—at "everyone who loved *Ficciones, In the Labyrinth,* or *Harmonium.*" Would the actual content of the novel, in such a context, acquire new meaning? I think so. I would be the first to fall for it. My review would read the narrative as an enormous metaphor for the search for epistemological certainty. If we grant this effect, then we must also grant that publishers' aiming other novels at the wide audiences for *Airport* or *Valley of the Dolls* dilutes or cheapens our estimation of these novels as literature. The frightening thing is that it may also lower their literary value in fact, if, as I fear, no one is keeping tabs on anything. Whole novels might be altogether lost. Why would a lover of literature pick up a novel aimed at readers of *Airport?* There must be many such novels every year, damned as both fish and fowl. I hope that a future army of graduate students will pore over ignored novels and rescue the literature, as *Moby-Dick* was rescued.

At any rate, the blurring of fictional genres keeps traditional virtues to the fore. Although we are certain that contemporary modernist fiction is, by intention, literature, nobody cares about these distinctions very much, and there is little pressure now on a writer to write it in order to be considered serious.

On the other hand, another exigency of the marketplace keeps fiction growing. Fortunately, I guess, the cry and clatter of forks is for young blood. The market requires new books. Poetry, music, and painting do not make much money until they are old. But for reasons I do not understand, people like to read their fiction before its ink has dried, and prefer the Book-of-the-Month Club to the public library. Since new writers are interested in expanding forms in fiction, many new books will necessarily exhibit new forms, and nudge fiction, and its recalcitrant audience, along.

Fiction's wide audience, its independence from dictatorial experts, and the sloppiness of its own literary definitions all keep the field lively, loose, and at the same time rooted in its own traditions. They keep it healthy. Other factors also keep fiction healthy in the same way, by contributing to the general confusion without unleashing mere anarchy.

Of these factors, none is more salutory than critical ambiguity about fiction's audience. Although we may call Jacqueline Susann a writer of entertainments and Anthony Powell a writer of literature, the relative size of their readership is not our basis for judgment. Although we look askance at any work which appeals to a very wide audience, we do not necessarily look away. We do not let audiences call the tune one way or the other.

A strange exception to this principle might be any critic who sees literature primarily as a cultural artifact. By these lights, a given narrative fulfills the unconscious wishes of a nation or a sex or it expresses the vision and needs of a social class. It follows that a Freudian or a Marxist critic would be intellectually inclined to pay particular attention to best sellers, on the grounds that these novels receive cultural sanctions precisely because they best express cultural norms. But these critics, I suggest, are not interested in literature for art's sake, and the concept of canon does not concern them.

In general, then, we not only refuse to fancy that all popular novels are good literature, we also refuse—

although less emphatically—to label them all bad. (Shakespeare, Dickens, and Tolstoy were popular, as are García Márquez, Pasternak, and Grass.) All this ambiguity amounts to this: fiction as a field, and even criticism, is almost free of the myth that plagues the plastic arts, that popular works are ipso facto bad. The stirring and true tales are at large of genuine artists, like the Impressionist and Post-Impressionist painters, or like Gerard Manley Hopkins, who lived in obscurity or ridicule and died in shame, while merely popular painters, whose works now fetch pennies, won their day. The idea is loose, I say, that popular work is bad, but it is not law, and it has not yet injured literary fiction.

On the other hand, it must make it almost impossible for painters to paint. How is one to guard against pleasing? If very popular painting is, by law, very bad, the painter, who is aiming at eternity, must insure against making his assault on eternity too attractive or available. For in one case, at least, popularity in the plastic arts amounted to a blackball. The example is Op Art. Lawrence Alloway of the Guggenheim has shown in an essay, "Notes on Op Art," how Op Art, in which he identifies fully respectable aesthetic intentions, was tarred and feathered by the art world before anyone thought about it, because advertising and business exploited the look in boutique fashions, teen magazine layouts, and dime store gear. Alloway cites, with venom, Thomas B. Hess's dismissal of Op Art in which Hess said that real painting is "difficult, serious, remote, aristocratic." Hess may be right. It is at any rate a memorable series of adjectives. But the poor "Op" painters were simply addressing real aesthetic issues, like any other painters. It is rough enough doing any art *sub specie aeternitatis* without asking

yourself every morning if your art is sufficiently aristocratic to be worth the candle, and sufficiently remote to
discourage all comers.

The French Impressionist bedtime story (which implies
that popular works are ipso facto bad) combines appall-
ingly with art's severing of historical ties to give contemporary painters the abysmal license of a free fall. Cut off
from both an audience and an agreed-upon set of traditional values, pushed out of a plane, a free-falling painter
may wiggle any way he chooses, repeating, "They
laughed at Manet and they laughed at Renoir"; but the
air is very thin. If the remote and aristocratic painter can
do no wrong, he can also do no right. And no one is
laughing now.

Another injurious idea of which literary critics and
writers are free is the notion, so damaging to the plastic
arts, that a work of art is produced only at some sort of
cutting edge of history. Wyndham Lewis called this notion "the demon of progress." By this account, the history
of art is a thin, wandering, and capricious line which
may intersect your studio or, more likely, miss it altogether. The artist, designated by hindsight, was the one
powerful enough, prophetic enough, or lucky enough to
swing that line his way. One might exaggerate further
and say this: that a given contemporary art object—say, a
painting—has artistic value not in itself, nor in relation to
enduring artistic values, but only in relation to the line.
(And it is a line, mind you, characterized by caprice. Who
can believe in it?) Contemporary objects are nothing in
themselves but potential objects of potential fate, waiting
until the moving finger writes and, having writ, moves
on. They are so many horses motionless at the gates. All

this means, to push an already overstated point, that the world of painting at any given moment consists of limbo objects on one hand and historical artifacts on the other: possible art, and former art (de La Tour, de Kooning) from former cutting edges.

It is hardly possible to exaggerate, in this respect, the importance of college curricula. Here we are at last: curricula. Put up your dukes.

Colleges and graduate schools educate both painters and writers; but art and literature curricula differ. Students infer from art history courses this notion of a cutting edge. Students can regard the history of art, like the history of science, as a series of innovations, or even corrections. Worse, they can see nineteenth- and twentieth-century art history as a series of liberations, as a systematic destruction of one barrier after another. How could those who become painters resist seeking the next barricade? In contemporary practice courses, students may paint grids or make mud huts; but they certainly realize that whatever the schools teach them is what is now and not what is next, and their only hope is to be next. The historical direction is abundantly clear. It moves from representation of the spiritual world to the secular world, from the secular world to increasingly abstracted forms, and from abstract forms to idea bare. But the line narrows, and it travels only forward. And there is nowhere to go from here.

On the other hand, literature as it is taught is scarcely the history of innovations. In fact it is, alas, scarcely even history at all. English departments are just as likely to teach literature generically as historically. Students may read ballads, Pope, and Yeats in the same week and learn to regard them all on the same plane. Even epic poetry may be taught simply as poetry. The novel is a genre; so is the short story. It is standard practice in fiction writing courses for students to read short stories by Tillie Olsen and Robert Coover alongside those by Turgenev and Melville; nobody bats an eye. Art history, by contrast, has no altarpiece courses.

Literature courses do not stress innovations; they stress texts. I have in fact an unexamined impression, which is surely not true and equally as surely not important, that Shakespeare made no innovations whatever. But a standard art history text lists an even dozen for Rembrandt. Even survey courses may come at history all cockeyed. In 1964, the first week of our sophomore literature survey took us directly from "Heart of Darkness" to *Sir Gawain and the Green Knight*. Art history is actually chronological history; a syllabus would not jump from Goya to Byzantine mosaics. I am by no means applauding any curricular trend away from the teaching of literature's history—quite the contrary. I mean only to suggest, ducking, that the decreased emphasis on historical survey courses could, theoretically, influence future writers and only future writers for the good. From any curriculum which stresses close textual scrutiny over chronological history, students infer that it is the task of writers in every generation to produce coherent texts—not to jump on a bandwagon or lead a charge.

Fiction as a field, however, is not suffering a crisis in the damaging-myth department. Of damaging myths there is no shortage whatever. Sometimes it seems as though the notion that art is expression is winning, or the notion that art is social documentation, or that art is over. People still magically regard novelists as helpless, fascinating neurotics who compose in deliriums or trances; the younger critics may regard them as even less conscious automatons who jerkily pace out the myths of their tribe; and the older critics do not regard them at all until they are dead. Young writers may be misled into thinking that novelists are rich or even that they are active. But this is silly.

More serious a threat is this notion: that quality will out, that quality has already outed, and that the novelists of whom we have heard are the novelists we have. People who believe this pronounce early and dismal verdicts: no one is writing interesting novels, or great novels, or great poetry, or great short stories. Which is absurd. How do we know who is writing what out there? Could Faulkner find a publisher now?

That we are much informed does not mean that we are well informed. What little contemporary criticism we have is responsible, but it must rely on what is available and even on what is expected. The *Times* could scarcely assign stringers, who also happen to be literary critics, to every garret and kitchen table in the country where the mute, inglorious Miltons are churning it out. And if the *Times* assigned such stringers, where would it print their reports, when it devotes breathless pages each week to the signing of blockbusters, jogging books, dieting books, and so forth? (It is hard to see whence arises the fuss about these objects whose share of the gross national product surely does not approach that of, say, bananas, or measuring cups—the details of whose marketing coups we are spared—unless someone really fancies that these leafy paper products borrow respectability from literary works on the flimsy coincidence that all are "books," or unless even a small sum of book money has a *creatio ex nihilo* charm to it that a great sum of banana money does not.)

At any rate, the fact that the growth of the art of literature is largely dependent upon the book industry makes for hard feelings all around. And it is here that the blurring of genres goes too far for art's health. From the viewpoint of big business, a dog care manual and a novel of genius are both marketable objects called "books"; since the dog care manual will be easier to market for profit, there is no point in taking a chance on the novel. This makes perfect sense. Every few dozen dog care manuals can, and do, fund a novel. But the offices are increasingly geared to the manuals, and decreasingly geared to literary fiction—which is sad for literature. So long as publishing is an industry among industries, the prestige of whose executives depends on profits, it will wish to publish literature, especially very original literature, only as an expensive, if beloved, hobby. Publishers, they say, deplore this state of affairs as much as anyone, wringing their hands all the way to the bank. Fortunately the prestige of publishing executives still depends a little bit on the literary quality of their lists; and fortunately the industry still harbors men and women who love literature and who try to move mountains in order to see it into print and even, at times, to ensure its promotion.

This is an old lovers' quarrel, the bitterer on the writers' side because ours is the greater dependency. Lord Byron, for instance, received an extravagantly printed Bible as a gift from his publisher John Murray. Byron sent the Bible back to Murray with a single emendation. At John 18:40, where the King James Bible read "Now Barabbas was a robber," Byron had changed the text to read "Now Barabbas was a publisher."

CHAPTER 6

Who Listens to Critics?

What effect has criticism on the direction of fiction? Is its influence conservative or innovative?

The question itself needs defending. For who in this country listens to critics? Are not the critics, off in their departmental corners, uselessly employed, changing their terms every few decades out of sheer boredom? Surely real fiction writers have no truck with academic critics, nor with any school but the school of hard knocks.

The notion of the novelist as gifted savage dies hard, even in English departments. (Perhaps it dies hard *especially* in English departments—for if Faulkner was a man of letters like thee and me, why have we not written great novels? Further, department scholars may doubt their own methods, their students, and especially their colleagues so much that they deny that anyone ever connected with that world could produce a novel worth reading.) It breaks our American hearts to learn that Updike was an English major. We wish to forget that Thoreau, like Updike and Mailer, was graduated from Harvard, and that Walt Whitman spent his life in his room studying and rewriting, and that Willa Cather lived among the literati in Greenwich Village, and that Melville left the sea at twenty-five. The will to believe in the fiction writer as Paul Bunyan is shockingly strong; it is emotional, like the will to believe in Bigfoot, the hairy primate who stalks the Western hills, or in the Loch Ness Monster. In fact, by the time the media had worked on Hemingway, he was scarcely distinguishable from Bigfoot, or less popular—and Dylan Thomas, that sentimental favorite, was the Loch Ness Monster. The assumption that the fiction writer is any sort of person but one whose formal education actually taught him something is particularly strong in this country; our democratic anti-intellectual tradition and our media cult of personality dovetail on this point and press it home, usually with full cooperation from writers.

In opposition to all this romance, I say that academic literary criticism is very influential: students listen to critics. What student does not read fiction for one course or another? And who is writing fiction these days who has not been to college?

For years on end the future fiction writer listens to Ph.D.'s, people professionally trained to approach texts using one method or another. It stands to reason that any critical approach which dominates the graduate schools will also dominate undergraduate thinking about fiction, such as it is, and will be felt, either positively or negatively, in the fiction those undergraduates will eventually write. Whether all this academic influence is baleful or not is another matter; the influence is real.

Well, then, how does academic criticism influence fiction's direction? Specific critical works, of course, have less effect than critical trends, which in turn are not so important as the fact of criticism itself and the milieu of self-consciousness that fact generates. For it is the nature of all the arts in this century to exist alongside criticism: alongside critical theory and history on one hand, and formal analysis on the other.

Let us say first that criticism keeps fiction traditional in several ways. As it influences curricula it most often defends the notion of canon and keeps students reading Trollope and Fielding, Hardy and Dickens, Cooper and Hawthorne. Students also study Joyce, Faulkner, and Woolf in the classroom, but they usually read Nabokov and Pynchon on their own, just as our professors a generation ago read Joyce on the sly. Further, English departments are usually stuck teaching solely literature written in English. This is so because modern language departments, in an understandable fight for their lives, may insist that students need German to read Kafka, French to read Proust, and Spanish to read Borges. English students may therefore lack genuine knowledge of European and Latin American fiction—which is far more modernist than British and American fiction—and so be graduated with a quaint and lopsided notion of the work done in this century. Finally, insofar as critical journals, as well as curricula, ignore contemporary fiction altogether, they may give the impression that anything written in our time is not interesting.

Criticism could encourage the stronghold of traditional

fiction in another, more complex way. Literary criticism, for all its changing terms and emphases, has a real continuity. Samuel Johnson's readings of Cowley and Shakespeare are still valuable; T. S. Eliot admired them enormously. And Eliot's readings of the English metaphysical poets and the French symbolist poets are still standard. Inversely, various modern critical methods work well on texts from any century—even on myth and folk tale. And when criticism does address itself to contemporary modernist fiction, it does not need a new language. A critic may intelligently apply to even the most experimental novel the same terms and methods he uses on *Pamela*. Nowhere do you find a set of critical tools appropriate only to a specific historical period.

Students absorb a sense of this critical continuity, and infer from it, as may we, that fiction as an art is proceeding along a bumpy but contiguous route to do what it has always done. This idea, in turn, devalues innovation per se, and allows respectability to older forms.

Art criticism, on the other hand, underwent a real crisis prompted by the radicality and swiftness of developments in the plastic arts. In even the most radical fiction of 1980, we have no departures so radical, in work or in theory, as the plastic arts had as long ago as 1910, 1911, 1912, and 1913, in Kandinsky, Kupka, Duchamp, and Malevich. The critical crisis was in full swing during the heyday of Abstract Expressionism. In 1962, for instance, leading critic Dore Ashton wrote: "No one has developed a rhetoric for criticism of abstract painting." Faced with the terms the painters themselves used for their methods and goals—paroxysm, delirium, orgasm, somnambulism, risk—critics could either soberly elucidate these misty nouns or go scrabbling for more nouns in the sticky realms of quantum mechanics, Taoism, Zen Buddhism, or Jung. The old terms suitable to figurative painting did not apply—because the multiple objects which figurative artists painted, and which figurative artists today continue to paint, are not merely incidental clothing of forms but genuine iconic subject matter. And the merest leaf or numeral in the corner of a painting permits critics to discuss the work as an interpretation of nature or of culture; its absence prohibits it.

Students may infer from painting's critical disarray that painting as a whole underwent a revolution in this century. Literature did not. Painting has "before" and "after" periods; literature does not. Young painters must look forward; young writers may look around.

Still, there are plenty of ways in which literary criticism encourages contemporary modernism. To return to canon: no writers are more firmly canonized than the historical Modernists. There is no shortage of critical attention to Faulkner or Woolf, say, or to Yeats or Stevens. And when curricula do teach literary history, they may talk about innovation; the present overblown reputation of *Ulysses* rests on its historical innovations.

More to the point is this: any formalist textual exegesis at all, whether it be Russian formalist, New Critical, phenomenologist, or structuralist, incidentally forwards contemporary modernist virtues. Such an exegesis stresses self-reference by limiting discussion to the text; it stresses ingenuity and pattern by tracing the visible patterns of structure and detail; and it stresses structural tautness by focusing on those materials which fit the analysis at the expense of those materials which do not fit. Dickens may fret a great deal about the engaging qualities of his work:

will they like this character? Is this description vivid? Will this scene wring their hearts? But formal criticism, outside of vague and personal British appreciations, cannot and does not analyze or quantify these effects. Emotional impact and simplicity are two virtues which traditional fiction may possess but which nevertheless strike textual criticism dumb.

Markedly characteristic of contemporary modernist fiction is its awareness of criticism. Any published criticism at all fuels these fires. Self-consciousness may be a handicap or a virtue; in either case, it is nothing new for writers. In 1818, John Keats was aware of the haunting demands on the writer which criticism and the weight of literary history made; but Keats "internalized" those demands, overcame his self-consciousness, and produced work from which both the writer and the critic were absent as figures. For the contemporary modernist, however, the same self-consciousness is inescapable. Art itself is the theme, and ironic, self-aware surfaces are the method: so the writer takes no pains to conceal his jitters.

Barth's stories "Lost in the Funhouse" and "Life Story" tremble with the sense of being read critically and analyzed; their protagonists are writers almost gibbering with witty self-consciousness. So is the protagonist in Beckett's trilogy *Molloy/ Malone Dies/ The Unnamable;* when he can overcome his paralysis sufficiently to write at all, he writes his novel defensively, against a host of critical readings. Some fiction parodies the critical essay: Nabokov's *Pale Fire,* Woody Allen's "Lovborg's Women Considered," Borges's "Pierre Menard, Author of Don Quixote." Today's writers are conscious of literary criticism indeed, if they know it well enough to parody it. It is not unreasonable to suppose that a familiarity with critical methods would make writers wish to produce texts which yield to, and fit, critical analysis.

On every continent, contemporary modernist fiction is written by educated and sophisticated writers. By no means all educated writers prefer it; but nowhere do uneducated writers produce it. (The many small biographies which Barbara Howes provides for her excellent anthology of Latin American short stories, *The Eye of the Heart*, bears out this correlation.) How could they? Borges is a library; Ronald Sukenick started out as a Wallace Stevens critic. But the charcoal burner who quits his vines and retires untutored to a garret will not invent contemporary modernism and will not like it when he sees it, any more than most undergraduates do. It is a taste acquired through cheerful familiarity with the provisional nature of literary texts and the relative nature of historical values. Of course, this degree of sophistication, like any sophistication in any field, inclines one to irony, jadedness, and cynicism with respect to received impressions on one hand, and to formalism, emotional caution, and self-consciousness with respect to personal expression on the other hand. But that's the breaks.

I would even like to proffer, as a spur to real investigation, the notion that awareness of criticism *created* contemporary modernist fiction. Contemporary modernist fiction arose among intellectuals in response to formalist critical ideals which have dominated the century: the ideals of the Russian formalists and the new Critics. (Phenomenologists and structuralists, heirs to this tradition, are too recent to have schooled a generation of writers.) Robert Scholes (*Structuralism in Literature*) has pointed out how the Russian formalists, who flourished 1915–1930, anticipated the fiction of Borges and Barth, fiction whose author's presence makes his narration subject to playful irony. Their notions sound contemporary modernist, and we could make a case for their direct or indirect influence on the young Russian Nabokov. On the other hand, perhaps we need not invoke Nabokov as a human vector for carrying formalist ideas to the United States. The publicity surrounding *Ulysses* was doing a good job of it, as were developments in the other arts, especially poetry.

The New Criticism arose in America in response to Modernist poetry in English—in response to the difficult, fragmented, and self-relevant poems of Eliot, Pound, Yeats, and Stevens. The New Critics were themselves poets to a man: Eliot, Pound, R. P. Blackmur, John Crowe Ransom, Allen Tate, William Empson, Kenneth Burke. They codified and bruited about the highly developed aesthetic of Modernist poetry; they introduced into the intellectual milieu, and into the classroom, the notion of texts as carefully patterned intellectual artifices. How could this not affect a generation of fiction writers? After you have performed or read a detailed analysis of Eliot's "Four Quartets" and Stevens's "Comedian as the Letter C," why would you care to write fiction like Jack London's or Theodore Dreiser's? Contemporary fiction writers may be more influenced by Pound's criticism than by Joyce's novels, more by Stevens's poems than Kafka's stories. In style their work more closely resembles "The Waste Land" than *Herzog*; in structure it more closely resembles "Thirteen Ways of Looking at a Blackbird" than *The Naked and the Dead*. This strand of contemporary fiction has purified itself through the agent of criticism; it has adopted the brilliant virtues of Modernist poetry, whose bones are its beauty.

On the whole, then, criticism nudges fiction toward contemporary modernist values. Its stress on textual values and on theory, and the self-consciousness it breeds, outweigh the effect of its conservative stance toward canon.

Actually, the impact of criticism on literature is not nearly so great as it is on painting. For literature is not yet the special province of experts, as we have seen. Experts are not needed; we can approach any work except *Finnegans Wake* unarmed. Literary criticism is useful, but not needful. In this it is like any art. It moves along independently and harmlessly, fascinated with and despairing of its own techniques, advancing by leaps and bounds into the empyrean. As an art form criticism is more highly developed than fiction is. Its own theories are actually the most suitable objects of its intelligence.

Painting's audience needs art critics. Anything interesting on earth will occasion many words, and when the words do not immediately suggest themselves, someone will propose them. Some painters themselves, even, may need art critics, not only to aid their own careers in the marketplace, but also to articulate a set of terms with which to disagree. The literature of Abstract Expressionism, for instance, is a catalogue of the painters' acrophobia and vertigo. They knew that much of their paintings' real action occurred in the realm where terms empty, analysis stammers, and judgment gapes. If someone is doing something that cannot be put into words, what, precisely, is he doing? The press wanted to know.

If you read six histories of Abstract Expressionism, you will read six accounts of the enormous influence of Harold Rosenberg and Clement Greenberg. The social art world befriends critics much more than the social literary world does. Literary criticism has some great figures, but none analogous to Rosenberg and Greenberg, whose criticism grew up alongside the painting, who introduced the art to the world and suggested some terms by which it could be discussed, and who arguably influenced the art itself.

CHAPTER 7

Fine Writing, Cranks, and the New Morality: Prose Styles

W_e hear many complaints about contemporary fiction—that its characters are flat and its stories are dull—but we hear no complaints about prose style. For in fact, prose styles have been one of the great strengths of Western fiction throughout this century. Prose style in fiction is like surface handling in painting. No matter how much people complain that contemporary works are saying little, no one denies that they say it very well.

We may distinguish among contemporary prose styles two overlapping strands. One is what we might for the moment call plain, the other fancy. Neither of these prose styles is distinctively, diagnostically modernist in the contemporary sense. Any sort of writer may use any sort of prose. But the fancy styles, in particular, may further modernist intentions by calling attention to themselves.

Shooting the Agate

Many contemporary prose styles derive from the mainstream of traditional fine writing. Fine writing, like painterly painting, has always been with us. We will, I hope, never cease to admire it. The great prose stylists of the recent past, until Flaubert, were fine writers to a man. A surprising number of these—those I think of first, in fact—wrote nonfiction: Robert Burton, Sir Thomas Browne, Samuel Johnson, Thomas De Quincey, Thomas Macaulay, Ralph Waldo Emerson, John Ruskin, William James, Sir James Frazer.

Who were the grand stylists of eighteenth- and nineteenth-century fiction? There is the lovely Turgenev and the brilliant Gorky, if we are to believe their translators; Melville had a rare strength; Hardy can be wholly limpid; Dickens is often rhythmic and powerful. But we do not think of any of these, except Turgenev, as great stylists—although we wrong Dickens not to. Who else? Stendhal? Chateaubriand? I think fine writing in fictional prose comes into its own only with the Modernists: first with James, and with Proust, Faulkner, Beckett, Woolf, Kafka, and the lavish Joyce of the novels.

This is an elaborated, painterly prose. It raids the world for materials to build sentences. It fabricates a semi-opaque weft of language. It is a spendthrift prose, and a prose of means. It is dense in objects which pester the senses. It hauls in visual imagery of every sort; it strews metaphors about, and bald similes, and allusions to every realm. It does not shy from adjectives, nor even from adverbs. It traffics in parallel structures and repetitions; it indulges in assonance and alliteration. Here is a splendid sentence from Ruskin:

> Every alteration of the features of nature has its origin either in powerless indolence or blind audacity, in the folly which forgets, or in the insolence which desecrates, works which it is the pride of angels to know, and their privilege to love.
>
> —Preface to *Modern Painters*, 2nd edition

The sentences of this prose may be very long, heavily punctuated throughout, and welded together with semicolons. Its lexicon is enormously wide, its spheres of reference global. We think of it as decorous, but actually it is not. Those old men in frock coats were after power, and power they got, by going for the throat. (Far more decorous is plain writing, the prose of Hemingway, Chekhov, and other stylists in shirts, who carefully limit their descriptions to matters at hand, and who produce a prose purified by its submission to the world.) There is nothing decorous about calling attention to yourself:

> The world is a Dancer; it is a Rosary; it is a Torrent; it is a Boat; a Mist; a Spider's Snare; it is what you will; and the metaphor will hold. . . . Must I call the heaven and the earth a maypole and country fair with booths, or an anthill, or an old coat, in order to give you the shock of pleasure which the imagination loves and the sense of spiritual greatness?
>
> —Emerson, *Journals*

Fine writing, with its elaborated imagery and powerful rhythms, has the beauty of both complexity and grandeur. It also has as its distinction a magnificent power to penetrate. It can penetrate precisely because, and only because, it lays no claims to precision. It is an energy. It sacrifices perfect control to the ambition to mean. It can penetrate very deep, piling object upon object to build a tower from which to breach the sky; it can enter with courage or bravura those fearsome realms where the end products of art meet the end products of thought, and where perfect clarity is not possible. Fine writing is not a mirror, not a window, not a document, not a surgical tool. It is an artifact and an achievement; it is at once an exploratory craft and the planet it attains; it is a testimony to the possibility of the beauty and penetration of written language.

Clearly, we are in the presence of a paradox here. How can prose be said to penetrate and dazzle? How can it call attention to itself, waving its arms as it were, while performing metaphysics behind its back? But this is what all art does, or at least all art that conceives of the center of things as insubstantial: as mental or spiritual. Fine prose in this sense is like Shakespeare's dramatic poetry, or Milton's epic poetry, or even Homer's. If you scratch an event, you get an idea. Fine writing does not actually penetrate the world of familiar things so much as it penetrates what, for lack of a better term, we might call the universe or even the realm of ideas. That is, this language does not penetrate things so much as it bears them away with it.

Shakespeare does not analyze Lear, or enter Lear. There was no Lear. Had there been a Lear, we could only say that Shakespeare transmogrified Lear. Lear, like Melville's whale, is an aesthetic or epistemological probe by means of which the artist analyzes the universe. When you really penetrate the world of things, as I understand the world of things, you encounter idea. And art, especially poetry and twentieth-century painting and fiction, objectifies idea on its own surface, by imitating thereon, in bits of world, the complex way that bits of mind cohere.

We have seen in twentieth-century painting that the art of mind and the art of surface go together. When painters abandoned narrative deep space, their canvases became abstract and intellectualized. With its multiple metaphors and colliding images, an embellished language actually abstracts the world's objects. Such language wrests objects from their familiar contexts. We do not enter deep space; we do not enter rounded characters; we contemplate them as objects. And when an artist both powerfully "realizes" his objects, rendering them in full material detail, and simultaneously "abstracts" them, rendering them under the aspect of eternity, then we may say that he penetrates these objects not to their specific, material hearts, but as it were out the other side, to their generalized forms, their created capacity to mean. He runs them through and hauls them off to heaven. Shakespeare does it with Lear; Cézanne does it with Mont Sainte Victoire. Paradoxically, an artist does all this on the surface, by the studied application of materials. He tacks his objects to the sky, either by baring their flattening forms, as Cézanne does, or, as Shakespeare does, by spiriting the objects out of the world with a hundred flights of language never heard.

At any rate, in this century even the illusion of penetration may no longer be the fine writer's intention. A fine writer may now, as in the eighteenth century, be ironic or playful as well as sincere. He may brandish his wealth of beauties to engage us or to dazzle us, to recreate a world or to embellish a surface. Fine writing is still with us. Density, even lushness, and elegance, forceful rhythms, dramatically fused imagery, and a degree of metaphorical splendor—these qualities still obtain and are the hallmark of fine writing. Included in this category are the rich collages of Joyce, where modernist fiction begins. Also included are the brittle sarcasms of Nabokov, and his much-wrought tendernesses, and especially his cryptographs—those challenges to literary criticism and parodies of its finds which are such red herrings to young writers, who must be relieved endlessly of the notion that the critic's role is to "find the hidden meaning" and the writer's role is to hide them, like Easter eggs. Here in this generalized category of fine writing also belong the poignant lyricisms of Beckett, the surrealisms of Gabriel García Márquez, the traditional elegances of Richard Hughes, E. M. Forster, and Joyce Cary, and the prose of many excellent and traditionalist Americans, like John Updike and William Gass. This is Gass: "The sun looks, through the mist, like a plum on the tree of heaven, or a bruise on the slope of your belly. Which? The grass crawls with frost."

Two subspecies of fine writing are particularly suited to modernist and contemporary modernist ends. One is a prose style so intimate, and so often used in the first person, that it is actually a voice. The voice appears in Europe throughout this century, and particularly between the wars. One could argue that it appeared in Eastern Europe and worked its way westward. It is the voice of a crank narrator. You hear it a bit in Gogol, and in Dostoevsky; you hear it especially in Kafka; you hear it in Elias Canetti, Witold Gombrowicz, Knut Hamsun, and now in Beckett, and Nabokov (*Despair, Pale Fire*).

This crank narrator is an enraged petty clerk, or a starveling, or a genius, or a monomaniac, or any sort of crazy. His is not an especially adult voice. He specializes in mood shifts. His voice is poetic, bellicose, and resigned. It deals in ironies, self-deprecations, arrogances, apologies, aggressions, whinings, obscenities, lyricisms, abrupt silences, flights of transcendence, and tantrums. This tone's energy depends, of course, on the rapid juxtaposition of these disparate moods—particularly a lyric mood interrupted by a note of aggrievement. Samuel Beckett has written three great novels using this one trick. The fact of the sky, in particular, seems to call forth the essence of this prose style. In *Molloy*, Beckett writes: "The sky was that horrible colour which heralds dawn." In *Ferdydurke*, Gombrowicz writes: "The sky, suspended in the heights, was light, fresh, pale, and sarcastic."

The crank narrator is a character outside bourgeois European culture; so is his creator. These writers either derive from peripheral countries, or are Jewish, or émigré, or are in some other way denied social access to mainstream European culture. One could easily argue that this culture itself disintegrated early in the century, and now everyone is adrift: this would account for the curiously contemporary sound of the voice. You may recognize the following as an imitation of Woody Allen, but it is not:

> Unparalleled cunning, great honesty of thought, and intelligence sharpened to a degree, will be required to enable man to escape from his stiff exteri-

or and succeed in better reconciling order with disorder, form with the formless, maturity with eternal
and sacred immaturity. In the meantime, tell me
which you prefer, red peppers or fresh cucumbers?

This is another passage from Gombrowicz's *Ferdydurke*,
which appeared in Poland in 1937 and caused a scandal.
Now everyone has caught the sound of this sort of mood-
shifting prose. It has moved from the provinces and ghet-
tos of Eastern Europe to New York City; now graduate
students in writing and comedians can reel it out like
yard goods.

The voice of the crank narrator is modernist in its distance, irony, and alienation; it is a mood composed of
many shifting moods. Another subspecies of fine writing
is even more contemporary. I have no name for this. It is
a dense extreme of fine writing, and it is diagnostically
contemporary modernist.

This prose repeats a fiction's narrative collage in a surface collage. Word by word, sentence by sentence, paragraph by paragraph, it proceeds by the same leaping
transitions and bizarre juxtapositions of voice, diction,
and image as the fiction as a whole does. It may use the
present tense: he walks, he remembers his father, his father is running. This flattens time and lends a floating,
objectlike quality to the narrative. (Oddly, the eighteenth-
century novelists used the present tense for immediacy.
Now we have learned to use it for distance.) This prose is,
above all, a wrought verbal surface. It changes subjects as
often as it changes moods; it presents us with an array of
all the world's objects moving so fast they spin. It whirls
us on a tour of the world of language. It does not pause to
examine any object; the verbal surface is itself the object.

I exaggerate; but the direction is there. Here is an example from a recent issue of *TriQuarterly*:

> In the jungle of language iridescent parrots and stern anchorites flash through the visual screen of the observer out to divine the scientific laws of the organic continuum that speaks in an infinity of frequencies ranging from a strident Squawk! to the smoothly radiating ripples in a pool.
> —John Bátki, "the footnote as medium"

Writers of such modernist prose may use the stream of consciousness convention to enhance the collage effect. Early stream of consciousness writers—Dorothy Richardson and Virginia Woolf, and perhaps Joyce, and Tillie Olsen today—use a disjunctive, imagistic, irrational prose in order, I think, to describe human experience as intimately and accurately as possible. Both intimacy and accuracy are traditional goals for fiction. Today some writers who use stream of consciousness technique (Burroughs, Beckett) use it for contemporary modernist ends. They intend, I think, to write neither intimately nor accurately. Instead, they may use interior monologue to unify and to justify the surface collage of language. Here is a fragment from Beckett's *How It Is:*

> my life a voice without quaqua on all sides word-scraps then nothing then again more words more scraps the same ill-spoken ill-heard then nothing vast stretch of time then in me in the vault bone-white if there were a light bits and scraps ten seconds fifteen seconds ill-heard ill-murmured ill-heard ill-recorded my whole life a gibberish garbled sixfold.

All these blithers and leaps are going on in somebody's

mind. It makes sense for the writer; it enables prose surfaces to be as rich and broken as cubist surfaces without sacrificing a narrative occasion.

I should mention here that contemporary modernist fiction has two major strands, and that these are never farther apart than here, over this matter of stream of consciousness. The aesthetics of surfaces and the aesthetics of distance do not always coincide. Modernist writers who use stream of consciousness today are most likely making prose objects; they are fabricating detailed canvases composed of fractured and reflecting bits. This is certainly contemporary modernist. But it is also contemporary modernist to emphasize intellectual structures, to dabble less in language than in metaphysics, and to handle characters and events from a great authorial distance, as if with tongs. Here we have Borges and Nabokov. And Borges and Nabokov despise stream of consciousness prose, almost as much as they despise Freud. It was the cliché of the generation that preceded theirs, and generation follows generation in a rage. For Borges and Nabokov, and perhaps for many of us raised on New Criticism, stream of consciousness prose, while it ranks among respectable techniques, is nevertheless suspect by virtue of its perilous proximity to matters subconscious, which in turn are entirely contaminated by the enthusiastic attention of amateurs.

The extreme among these dense modernist prose styles gives a clotted, impasto effect. It slathers an almost opaque layer of language between the reader and the world. The Beckett passage I just quoted falls into this category. Here is another passage, from William Burroughs's "a distant hand lifted." Burroughs wrote that he meant this prose to "approximate walky talky immediacy so that the writer writes in present time." The subject matter here is what he calls "random impressions from whatever is presented to [the writer] at the moment." Here goes:

> "You/and I/sad old/broken film/knife/cough/it lands in/cough/present time/long cough/decoding arrest/ wasn't it?:::::::cough/immediacy/cough/empty arteries must tell you/cough/'adios'/who else?/ cough/drew Sept. 17, 1899/over New York???

A very self-conscious, hammering prose is difficult to sustain over the length of a novel. Even if the writer can keep hammering, the reader may not wish to be hammered at for so long. A writer does well to unify a dense prose with a voice. An English writer named Nik Cohn wrote a novel using such an opaque voice. The novel, *Arfur*, published in England in the mid 1970's, combined the rhythms of a rarefied New Orleans jazz slang with the vocabulary of pinball (!) to create a rich and brilliant piece of fine writing. He refers to "a very mosey style of walk, adopted off the riverboats, known as shooting the agate." "Willie the Pleaser," he writes, "he was a cheat without equal, and he taught me many strokes, how to flare, how to float, how to flick from the elbow, so that I became expert in all the paths of subterfuge." Without the unity of a voice, a very dense prose can be rough going, especially in a novel. It may be emotionally overwrought, as in the work of Edward Dahlberg, or it may be distant and bristling. The prose of the first thirty pages of Nabokov's *Ada*, for instance, is a barrage of language released from occasion; it is a breastwork of puns and cryptic allusions which effectively defend the novel's contents from the reader's interest—until Nabokov is good and ready.

Very often we find an especially dense and contemporary modernist fine prose style outside the novel. We find it in the short story, and especially in the very short story, the "prose piece" with which we have been lately overwhelmed. Published as fiction, works of the latter category are less often referred to as stories than as "pieces"—just as objects of contemporary art which are neither easel paintings nor formal sculptures are called pieces.

I think a theory of contemporary modernism could have predicted the burgeoning of these short prose objects, some of them so reminiscent of Rimbaud's *Illuminations*. After all, fiction in this century has been moving closer to poetry in every decade. These are shifting and refracting language surfaces whose affective subject matter is in large part their own surface technique. The authors of such works do not resort to the radical aesthetic experiments of Gertrude Stein; they do instead permit their language to refer to the world. But the world is so flattened and fragmented it becomes for the reader a kind of vivid and emotional memory in chips and dots which color the surface workings of the text. The world is finally almost buried in technique. The replacement of deep space with abstracted patterns of paint, and of felt events with semi-abstracted patterns of language, is an achievement of modern art. The technical surfaces of such works are pure. Their intentions can be only aesthetic. No sentimentality of subject matter interferes with their formal development. Their pleasure to the senses, and their attraction for the mind, may be considerable.

Contemporary American poets, incidentally, write some of the best of these short prose pieces: Jayne Anne Phillips, Mark Strand, W. S. Merwin. Donald Barthelme was writing them in the sixties. The works are disparate.

Each artist of course bends the form to his own vision. The works resemble each other only in length and in the polished and compacted ironies of their prose. Often the sentences are slower, more tense, and more imagistic than the sentences of contemporary poetry. As narratives they may be evocative or symbolic or relatively straight-forward. As descriptions they are often disturbing in their brutality, irrationality, sexuality, or sudden lyricism. Their mood may be at once evocative and mean. The writers of these prose pieces do not, I think, intend them to be deep and engaging as traditional short stories are deep and engaging. They are small objects composed of a glittering language cemented by reference. At their least significant they may be mere slices of language which startle, disturb, or titillate; at their best they are structured and patterned short pieces of fiction or description which display in small, and upon a flattened aesthetic surface, the coherence of art.

Fine writing, as I have said, need not be contemporary modernist in intention. A traditional fine writer like Updike handles his prose as a painterly painter handles paint—with it he describes, beautifully and suggestively, an object in the world. The object shapes the medium. By contrast, contemporary modernist fine writers wield their prose more aggressively. Their prose is not so much a descriptive tool as an end in itself. Raiding the world for fleeting images, they fabricate a prose impressionist and refracting, or moodily expressionistic, or fragmented, cryptic, and surreal.

Calling a Spade a Spade

Other twentieth-century writers avoid fine writing. Borges, for example, has disclaimed his early story "The

Circular Ruins" for its lush prose. Fine writing does indeed draw attention to a work's surface, and in that it furthers modernist aims. But at the same time it is pleasing, emotional, and engaging, like quondam beautiful effects with paint. It is literary. It is always vulnerable to the charge of sacrificing accuracy, or even integrity, to the more dubious value, beauty. For these reasons it may be, in the name of purity, jettisoned.

With Flaubert a new value for prose styles emerges. Prose must not be elaborate, at risk of being lacy. Instead, it should be, as the cliché goes, "honed to a bladelike edge." This is a new sort of beauty in prose. Verbal dazzle, after all, is almost universally attractive; nineteenth-century Europeans admired it enormously. It takes a sophisticated ear, even a jaded ear, to appreciate the beauty and integrity of a careful simplicity. I am thinking here of the prose of Flaubert, Chekhov, Turgenev, Sherwood Anderson, Hemingway, Paul Horgan, Wright Morris, Henry Green, Robbe-Grillet, and Borges.

This prose is, above all, clean. It is sparing in its use of adjectives and adverbs; it avoids relative clauses and fancy punctuation; it forswears exotic lexicons and attention-getting verbs; it eschews splendid metaphors and cultured allusions. Instead, it follows the dictum of William Carlos Williams: "no in ideas but in things."

Plain writing is by no means easy writing. The *mot juste* is an intellectual achievement. There is nothing relaxed about the pace of this prose; it is as restricted and taut as the pace of lyric poetry. The short sentences of plain prose have a good deal of blank space around them, as lines of lyric poetry do, and even as the abrupt utterances of Beckett characters do. They erupt against a backdrop of silence. These sentences are—in an extreme form of plain writing—objects themselves, objects which invite inspection and which flaunt their simplicity. One could even, if one were cynical, accuse such plain sentences of the snobbery of Bauhaus design, or of high tech furnishings, or of the unobtrusive suit: one could accuse them of ostentation. But I anticipate a theoretical flaw I have never encountered in fact. As it is actually used, this prose has one supreme function, which is not to call attention to itself, but to refer to the world.

This prose is not an end in itself, but a means. It is, then, a *useful* prose. Each writer of course uses it in a different way. Borges uses it straightforwardly, and as invisibly as he can, to think, to handle bare ideas with control:

> Hume denied the existence of an absolute space, in which each thing has its place; I deny the existence of one single time, in which all events are linked.
> —"A New Refutation of Time"

Robbe-Grillet uses it coldly and dryly, to alienate, to describe, and to lend his descriptions the illusion of scientific accuracy. His prose is a perceptual tool:

> ... the square occupying the table's left rear corner corresponds to the base of the brass lamp that now stands in the right corner: a square pedestal about one inch high capped by a disk of the same height supporting a fluted column at its center.
> —*In the Labyrinth*

Hemingway uses it like a ten-foot pole, to distance himself from events; he also uses it like chopsticks, to handle strong emotions without, in theory, becoming sticky: "On the other hand his father had the finest pair of eyes he had ever seen and Nick had loved him very much and for a long time." (At its worst, this flatness may be ludicrous. Hemingway once wrote, and discarded, the sentence "Paris is a nice town.")

Writers like Flaubert, Chekhov, Turgenev, Sherwood Anderson, Anthony Powell, and Wright Morris use this prose for many purposes: not only to control emotion, but also to build an imaginative world whose parts seem solidly actual and lighted, and to name the multiple aspects of experience one by one, with distance, and also with tenderness and respect. In two sentences I heard read aloud many years ago in a large auditorium, Wright Morris introduced me to the virtues of an unadorned prose. The two sentences were these: "The father talks to his son. The son listens and watches his father eat soup." (*Love Affair—A Venetian Journal*)

This prose is craftsmanlike. It possesses beauty and power without syntactical complexity. Because of its simplicity, writers use this prose to handle a certain kind of character—a character who does not belong in a drawing room, but is not meant to be seen as a picturesque rustic. Plain prose can follow such characters intimately, lovingly, even a little ironically, and always with respect. It is this which Wright Morris does so well. He writes a perfected prose of surpassing delicacy, control, and power. It is a fictional prose tied to character. It honors the world because the characters honor the world. Listen to these adjectives:

> Floyd Warner kept a calender on which he jotted
> what sort of day it was, every day of the year.
> Windy, overcast, drizzly, rain, clear and cool, clear
> and warm, and all through October he put simply,

Dandy. Practically every day was dandy, and that had been true over the years.

—*Fire Sermon*

This prose is a kind of literary vernacular. It possesses the virtues of beauty, clarity, and strength without embellishment.

In England, Henry Green also writes very often from the minds of people who are not formally educated and who know the world and love it on its merits. But Green's prose, unlike Morris's, is stylized to the point of self-consciousness. It is hard to know where to place Green's prose, a prose so plain it is distracting. Almost all experimental prose is a species of fine writing; Green's is experimental *plain* writing. At its quirkiest, it omits articles for the sake of concision, and sounds like Tonto: "Mr. Craigan smoked pipe, already room was blurred by smoke from it." The warped purity of such prose achieves a watercolor lyricism: "Just then Mr. Dupret in sleep, died, in sleep." "What happened of her. What did her come to?"

Plain prose is also good for comedy—as opposed to mere wit. Henry Green, Wright Morris, and Eudora Welty all use a vernacular prose to deadpan:

> "I," says Mama, "I prefer to take my children's word for anything when it's humanly possibly." You ought to see Mama, she weighs two hundred pounds and has real tiny feet.
> —Welty, "Why I Live at the P.O."

Finally, plain prose is almost requisite for handling violent or emotional scenes without eliciting dismay or nausea in the reader. We have long since tired of imitation fine writing, of bad fine writing, of the overwritten, gushing prose which we find not only in unskilled literature but also in junk fiction—and we tire of it especially in the wringingly emotional and violent scenes of which failed literature and junk are made. So unless he is William Faulkner, a serious writer of this century has little other recourse than to plain writing for violent and emotional scenes. If a writer wants to play safe, he will underwrite all drama. Plain prose affords distance; it permits scenes to be effective on their narrative virtues, not on the overwrought insistence of their author's prose. The central love scene of Powell's twelve-volume *A Dance to the Music of Time* ends unforgettably: "I took her in my arms."

There is something about plain writing which smacks of moral goodness. Interestingly, some writers turn to it more and more as they get older. There is a modesty to it. Paul Horgan uses three different plain prose styles in his Richard trilogy, a series of novels which take the form of autobiography. Henry Green uses plain prose in his autobiography. Graham Greene uses it in his autobiography. It is a mature prose. It honors the world. It is courteous. Its credo might be that of French entomologist J. Henri Fabre: "Lucidity is the sovereign politeness of the writer. I do my best to achieve it." Part of its politeness to readers is based on respect; this prose credits readers with feeling and intelligence. It does not explain events in all their ramifications; it does not color a scene emotionally so that a reader knows what he should feel.

This prose is humble. It does not call attention to itself but to the world. It is intimate with character; it is sympathetic and may be democratic. It submits to the world; it is honest. It praises the world by seeing it. It seems even to *believe* in the world it honors with so much careful attention. In the nineteenth century, readers liked their prose syntactically baroque and morally elevating. Each bit of world was a chip off the old sublime, and tended distressingly, in the prose which described it, to ascend to heaven before we got to know it.

> Nothing so fair, so pure, and at the same time so large, as a lake, perchance, lies on the surface of the earth. Sky water. It needs no fence. Nations come and go without defiling it. It is a mirror which no stone can crack, whose quicksilver will never wear off, whose gilding Nature continually repairs . . .
> —Thoreau, *Walden*

Our reaction to such ebullience is of course to reverse it. We have modern tastes and like writing which is precise and uncluttered. We are agnostic or materialist and like writing fastened to the world of things. This plain prose represents literature's new morality. It honors each thing one by one, without metaphor. No angelic systems need be dragged in by the hair to sprinkle upon objects a borrowed splendor. Instead, each of the world's unique objects is the site of its own truth and goodness. Each thing is its own context for meaning. Its virtue is its stubborn uniqueness, in its resistance to generalization, or even in its resistance to our final knowledge of it. The most general trend we know is speciation.

Plain prose can be polished to transparency without losing strength. At its best, its form follows its function so accurately that its very purity and hard-won simplicity excite our admiration almost in spite of themselves. It does not err on the side of exuberance. It does, *in theory,* win through to material "things as they are"—things seen without bias or motive. That can be its epistemological claim. And aesthetically it can claim control, purity, and the dignity of material essences. And it can claim the just precision of a tool, the spareness of bone, the clarity of light. Do not confuse these claims with the clichés of contemporary craftsmen in materials who labor to help you understand that a wooden spoon may have integrity, a wooden apple barrel may have dignity, a wooden bench simple functional beauty, so that you labor in turn to find some kindling and a match. There is nothing clichéd about clear prose yet. For all its virtues, fine writing may be a mere pyrotechnic display, dazzling and done. And plain writing is not a pyrotechnic display, but a lamp.

If we call very opaque modernist prose a painted sphere, and plain prose a clear windowpane, then we will see that these are extremes; most literary prose belongs somewhere in the middle. Or if we call fancy experimental prose "poetry" and plain prose "science," then again we will see that most prose falls somewhere in the middle. In this middle ground we have contemporaries like Borges and Ralph Ellison writing complex modernist fiction using straightforward prose. And we have writers like Tillie Olsen writing stories of intimacy and depth whose virtues are traditional, yet whose prose surfaces are nevertheless dislocated and modernist. Most frequently we have writers of traditional literature modified by this century's concerns, who use a beautiful and strong literary prose modified by this century's taste for flat and shifting surfaces. In England, for instance, a prose which is at once perfectly clean yet capable of stunning elegance still endears the writers of the last generation to mine: the prose of E. M. Forster and Joyce Cary on the elaborate side, and on the spare side, Henry Green and Anthony Powell.

The species of prose blur. Writers of course vary their modes from book to book. Sometimes even within a book—a book of short stories—we find radically different kinds of excellent prose bent to radically different and excellent ends. I am thinking here of Richard Selzer's *Rituals of Surgery*, of *Getting into Death* by New York writer Thomas M. Disch, and of *Beasts of the Southern Wild* by Carolina writer Doris Betts. Every mode is an option now. It is anybody's ball game.

Let me add this. You know how a puppy, when you point off in one direction for him, looks at your hand. It is hard to train him not to. The modernist arts in this century have gone to a great deal of trouble to *untrain* us readers, to force us to look at the hand. Contemporary modernist fine prose says, Look at my hand. Plain prose says, Look over there. But these are matters of emphasis. So long as words refer, the literary arts will continue to do two things at once, just as all representational painting does two things at once. They point to the world with a hand.

I think the very finest works of art do both things at once and well. Cézanne's still lifes and landscapes, for instance, depict. They push the paint surface into a modified simulation of deep space; the meadow tilts back toward the mountain. At the same time they pull deep space up toward the surface of the picture plane; the mountain looms flat against the canvas. The paintings' greatness depends on this spatial tension. Just so do artifice and sincerity meet and balance in a great work of art. We teeter at the edge of the artists' representations, affected by their depths and at the same time admiring their effects. Look at Shakespeare. Who could say where the greater power of *King Lear* resides? Do we enter it as an emotional world of enlarged sympathies wherein we lose ourselves? Or do we admire it more as an artifice of theater and language?

Finally, it is interesting to note Robbe-Grillet's peculiar notion (which I think is accurate) that a writer thinks of a future novel first as "a way of writing." The narrative, he says, "what will happen in the book [,] comes afterward, as though secreted by the style itself." This is interesting because it stresses again the primacy, for the modernist, of notions of surface treatment and handling. One does not *choose* a prose, or a handling of paint, as a fitting tool for a given task, the way one chooses a 5/16 wrench to loosen a 5/16 bolt. Rather—and rather creepily—the prose "secretes" the book. The narrative is a side effect of the prose, as our vision is a side effect of our seeing. Prose is a kind of cognitive tool which secretes its objects—as though a set of tools were to create the very engines it could enter, as though a wielded wrench, like a waved soap bubble wand, were to emit a trail of fitted bolts in its wake.

PART THREE

Does the World Have Meaning?

CHAPTER 8

The Hope of the Race

Octavio Paz points out that since the breakdown of religion and metaphysics, "we have criticism instead of ideas, methods instead of systems. Our only idea, in the proper sense of the term, is Criticism." The Myth of Criticism, he repeats, is *"the only modern idea."*

Depressing as the thought is, the myth of criticism is a workable myth, as powerful as any. Criticism is a kind of modern focusing of the religious impulse, the hope of the race: the faith that something has meaning, and we may apprehend it. Are we people given to know the meaning of something, even if it is only the tiny textual world fashioned by our neighbor? (If so, the mind will never run out of meaningful objects.) Art has meaning, which criticism discerns. This is a cheerful state of affairs, actually, but it obtains only if we grant that art actually does mean (a topic I will tackle presently) and also if we grant that criticism can know art.

May we entertain these hopes?

May We Discover Meaning?

Bear with me, please, for a few difficult points before the shooting starts. Readers who are not interested in the complex internal problems of literary criticism should skip directly to page 132 (Peirce); there, this chapter, and the book as a whole, begin to take off at last.

Certain contemporary critics, who might be called quasi-structuralists, hold that both texts and criticism are locked in "the prisonhouse of language" (the phrase is Nietzsche's), so that while criticism fails to refer meaningfully to anything, that is all right, because so does art. This view licenses the critic to perform all sorts of aerialist feats. It was with great good humor that Neil H. Hertz once provisionally titled an essay "Wordsworth's Influence on Milton." Of course, these critics deny the notion of influence and the notion of theme. All the universe is language, and language is self-referential. Critic Jeffrey Mehlman, in *Revolution and Repetition,* took a word which Freud used in a specific, quirky, and fully elaborated sense (*unheimlich*—uncanny), and "inscribed" Freud's meaning for that word back into an unrelated text by Marx. By this curious device, Mehlman produced, as one might expect, an ingenious and novel reading of the Marx text. (It is as if we were to take Psalm 121—"I will lift up mine eyes unto the hills, from whence cometh my help"—and read "the hills" as Ché Guevara might use the term.) If we complain that such artificial readings are merely playful or ingenious, that they are irresponsible because they do not *refer* to anything actual, these critics can reply that all mental effort and verbal artifact is artificial, playful, ingenious, and irresponsible.

This is an extreme position. Let us step down a notch to another position, which holds that while art may be meaningful within itself, the art object is always unknowable. Criticism must always try to know a text on its own terms; but it will always fail. Criticism cannot know its object. There is no guaranteed thread of connection between any interpretation and any text; so criticism is a particularly fanciful and baroque form of skywriting. Formalist critics, for instance, may hold that a text is wholly sealed. Its locked lights bat back and forth inside their can. Therefore, as Harold Bloom said once: "There are no interpretations but only misinterpretations, and so all criticism is prose poetry." In this context, "prose poetry" signifies a system coherent but detached, whose reference never overflows its pages and never meets any external object—world or text. And so criticism is blind and dreaming.

But this, too, is an extreme position which the embattled intellect cannot long defend. For it is simply too absurd to approach an object which you (and you alone) must define as unapproachable, and then to produce a careful interpretation of it which you must judge meaningless. Even the most depressive critic among us does not doubt, I think, that his interpretation is worth a little something. Why else would he teach it, write it, and defend it? And he does not really doubt, I think, that the text at hand leaks light all over creation. It may be reductive to say that *Othello* is about jealousy or that "The Emperor of Ice Cream" is about a funeral, but it is more reductive to say that these texts do not concern these things at all, nor do they touch anything whatever that we can name; and it is a mad exaggeration to say that the words of a text are runic, like so many dots of paint. We can interpret texts because texts use a shared language which refers, however clumsily, to a shared world. We may never *exhaust* the meaning of a text, or our knowledge even of its textual surface; but to acknowledge that we can never know all is not to decide that we can know nothing.

Further, any kind of critical interpretation may be sound and useful without being airtight or guaranteed. Must we say that we can never interpret? May we suggest that the crow and the dust of snow and the hemlock tree in Frost's little poem "Dust of Snow" are reminders of death? Or could we just as reliably hold that the crow and the snow and the hemlock are symbols of homosexual desire, or Yankee food taboos? Skepticism and the relativism it breeds are, in this case and as usual, nonsense. The fact that there are cases difficult to interpret within a given cultural context does not alter the fact that there are clearer cases. Criticism accumulates an ordered pile of sound work behind it just as physics does. (It could even be that criticism is on firmer ground than physics—because cultural phenomena occur on an accessible middle ground, and human fabrications fit human understanding.) The concepts of class, marketplace, and culture, for instance, are interpretative notions which have assumed the status of common "hard" knowledge, just as Freud's interpretative concepts have, and those of Malthus.

To judge among interpretations and methods, we must resort either to the authority of the author's stated intentions, if any, or to common sense, or to a consensus among educated people of goodwill. None of these satisfies anyone, but there is nothing else. Any effort to make of criticism an exact science necessarily limits its materials to only those things which can be known for certain—such as the number of times a given word occurs in an established text—and therefore evades criticism's interpretative function almost entirely. (Of course, criticism also contributes to knowledge high heaps of more or less undisputed data—data historical, biographical, and bibliographical. Such studies constitute a great part of criticism's business, but they are not at issue here except insofar as they may enlighten interpretations of texts.)

Say, then, that although criticism may produce solid and useful interpretations of texts, it can never test its methods or guarantee its findings. Is criticism then prose poetry? What can we say of criticism's many and excellent interpretations—J. Hillis Miller on *Bleak House*, Harold Bloom on "Byzantium," Northrop Frye on "Jerusalem"—that these readings are true? Or that they are, by consensus, probable, workable, and fruitful? We can say the latter. And that is good enough.

For on what ground do the other branches of knowledge stand? After all, there is no epistemological guarantee between *any* subject and *any* object. The world itself may be sealed. If we are talking about knowledge (holding interpretation at bay for the moment), criticism is on no swampier ground than any other branch of knowledge. It could be, even, that texts are a great deal *more* accessible to knowledge than other objects. At least we do not dispute that texts *exist*. Even when general debate stretches to the point where we doubt (or feign to doubt) that the world out there exists, any of it, we seldom if ever find our epistemological panic focused on the issue of texts. To vary a Woody Allen joke: It could be that the universe has no existence independent of our perceptions, that the universe is a fabrication of our dreaming senses—in which case I definitely overpaid for my copy of *Lord Jim*.

At any rate, even if the great world exists, there are ample reasons to deny that we can know it. The abyss between any subject and any object and the utter lack of any guaranteed relationship between them confronts anyone who thinks about anything. All possible knowledge, from the identification of species to the size of your foot, is necessarily interpretative. Inhibitors in our neurons edit the garbled impressions of our meager senses before they reach our programmed brains. All language-using endeavor is culturally purblind. So all our data are at best biased. At worst, we can know nothing. Profound epistemological skepticism and the blithe relativism which accompanies it are always intellectual options, or at least roles, and for anyone who assumes them, *all* the branches of knowledge are prose poetry.

But as C. S. Peirce wrote, perhaps sentimentally: "Let us not pretend to doubt in philosophy what we do not doubt in our hearts." We may well doubt that all things can be known or understood, but we do not really doubt that *some* things can be known and understood—or else we would neither argue nor teach our children. It is always instructive to ask a relativist how he raises his children.

Since we agree that some things can be known and understood, our human endeavor is to extend the boundaries of sense and meaning; it is to shift phenomena one by one out of the nonsense heap and arrange them in ordered piles about us. If you argue that this endeavor yields only a human kind of sense, and that our interpretations yield only human meanings, not absolute meanings, you will be required to propose a definition of meaning that is *not*, first and last, meaning for people.

If, as even the early skeptic Arcesilaus granted, we can obtain at best probable knowledge, that in itself is no mean feat. We have come a long way on probable knowledge. For Einstein, the final mystery of the universe was that we are able to know it. ("One may say that the eternal mystery of the world is its comprehensibility.") Our little human prose poems somehow connect to the mechanism. Einstein must have felt very queasy when the 1919 solar eclipse demonstrated that light does indeed bend in a gravitational field—a demonstration that corroborated general relativity and with it curved, inbounded space. He must have been dumbfounded, must have wanted to issue a telegraphed disclaimer to the universe: I WAS JUST KIDDING. For although we often feel pleased by the connections our minds make, we rarely, I think, feel they are absolutely true. (What if Chekhov went to heaven and God clapped him on the shoulder and said, "YOU WERE CORRECT"?)

Consider a tangential phenomenon. Opinion polls collect opinions, which are human judgments and interpretations. Opinion polls do not ask us to mark statements "true" or "false," but "agree" or "disagree." It could be that poll-takers would have a hard time finding any educated adult who would mark any interpretative statement "true." I would readily mark a number of statements "agree" which I would hesitate or refuse to mark "true"—even statements with which I may passionately concur. Do I agree with the Sermon on the Mount? (Yes.) Is it true? (?) Do I agree with this editorial about the presidential candidate? (Yes.) Is it true? (?)

Why is this so? It is a very interesting phenomenon,

and one which, from one point of view, casts higher education in a dubious light. I do not judge this hesitation peculiar to myself, but freely ascribe it to others: why do we say we agree with a proposition we will not call true? Is this, perchance, becoming modesty? Not likely. Is it then intellectual cowardice, or "healthy" skepticism, or simply hypocrisy? Which of these did we learn in school? Which do we teach?

I have worried these questions for some days and settled on a simple answer which disburdens us all of the labels coward and hypocrite, and which you knew all along: we do not ordinarily apply the criterion of truth to any interpretations whatever.

Is Linnaean classification true? Is Plato's metaphysic true? Physical scientists, of course, speak of an interpretation's being probable, or workable, or fruitful, just as critics do. Interpretations of data do not have the truth status of data themselves; nor are they, I think, intended to, which is why I attribute queasiness to Einstein, albeit jokingly. Physical interpretations and methodologies are debatable, just as critical ones are. To determine the "truth" of a given interpretation of physical data, we poll the experts. Even in mathematics, consensus is the final judge. Writing in *Scientific American*, Martin Gardner says: "The validity of a difficult proof rests on a consensus among experts, who may, after all, be mistaken." At this level the only status difference between a physical interpretation and a critical one is that new data will likely appear in, say, physics, altering as it were the world text, but it is unlikely that a substantially new literary text will replace the old one. In this way, too, criticism may be on firmer ground than physics.

Matters of scientific interpretation, then, are subject to

heated debate along the lines of "agree"/"disagree." The debate can come to blows. But when the terms change to "true" or "false," a curious hush descends on the ring. The blows cease and the air fills with disclaimers: gee, it's dark in here. Who turned out the lights? That is why science has so much trouble talking to the press; the press thinks in terms of "true" and "false." When the reporter, notebook in hand, enters the arena, the scientists who have been exchanging blows only seconds before now join hands and sing, "We cannot know. We are only fooling around." The same situation obtains in theology. At any rate, to worry that we can never call a given critical interpretation "true" is not to worry.

Who Is Crazy?

We may make an interesting distinction between two types of phenomena: those which we may know, and those which we may both know and understand in terms of meaning. For the hope of all criticism, and the hope of the race, is not only that we may know, but also that we may understand. Our understanding of meaning requires that things have meaning. Do things have meaning?

For a pantheist they do. To an Australian aboriginal before Europeanization, as is well known, every bush and rock, by its very existence, continuously uttered its human meaning as if it were speech. The desert was an elaborate and personal message, or a great book which people could read and interpret. Similarly, to superstitious people everywhere and at all times, events and objects are personal omens and portents and commands.

It has been many centuries since adult Europeans have enjoyed and feared a universe so sentient, so voluble, and so interested in their doings. Christianity and science, which on big issues go hand in hand intellectually as well as historically, everywhere raised the standard of living and cut down on the fun. Everywhere Christianity and science hushed the bushes and gagged the rocks. They razed the sacred groves, killed the priests, and drained the flow of meaning right off the planet. They built schools; they taught people to measure and add, to write, and to pray to an absent God. The direction of recent history is toward desacralization, the unhinging of materials from meaning. The function of Western knowledge is to "de-spookify." Christianity and early science began this process; the ideals of the Protestant Reformation and the Counter-Reformation, coupled with Enlightenment ideals of progress and democracy, carried it still further. The individual, with his society changing all around him, with his private prayer and reasoned vote, was the new unit of meaning.

From there to secular existentialism was but a single, natural step: you do not find or discover personal meaning in the world, nor do your unchanging social traditions dish it out, nor does your church. Instead, you make it up. You make it up from what is left, from internal elements alone, such as moods. The paucity of internal materials, you will find, leaves you free intellectually to range the whole gamut of relativism.

We can trace a progression, then, from the judgment that everything we see has meaning, to the judgment that nothing we see has meaning. Between these two extreme positions we have, believe it or not, criticism and the other interpretative fields, which assert that *some* things have meaning. Let us adopt this position: some things have meaning. The question now is: *which* things have meaning? Where do we draw the line?

Which things have meaning? Let us consider the stirring example of Hans Prinzhorn. Hans Prinzhorn is a psychotherapist who wrote *Artistry of the Mentally Ill*. Referring to the doodles, and only the doodles, of hospitalized schizophrenics, Prinzhorn asserted: "Even the smallest loop . . . can be understood . . . and interpreted." Happy Hans Prinzhorn! For he has found a method (presumably Freudian) for the finding of meaning in "even the smallest loop"! He will never run out of objects from which meaning can be derived, so long as schizophrenics keep doodling. In the happiness of his situation, and in the centrality of his position in the very thick of meaning, he is matched only by the schizophrenics on the other side of the desk, who were presumably hospitalized in the first place for, among other things, the creepy habit of finding meaning in even the smallest loop of everything.

"I know for a fact," said one patient, "that each tree has a habeas corpus in front of it. . . . The habeas corpus tells everything about that tree." "You'd be surprised," this patient said on another occasion, "how much cosmics cobwebs give off." Very busy in another asylum was an artist, Adolf Wölfli. Wölfli, a child-molester who spent the last thirteen years of his life in isolation from other asylum inmates, made elaborate drawings and paintings dense with meanings. (He conceived of a highest number called Oberon, "which may not be surpassed, at the risk of catastrophe.") Of his work he said brightly, "There is so much to do here. You'd never guess how you have to use your head so as not to forget anything. It would be enough to drive a body mad if he wasn't mad already."

Schematically we could see an asylum as a meaning factory. The schizophrenics understand and interpret the world's smallest loops; the schizophrenics doodle. Hans Prinzhorn understands and interprets the schizophrenics' doodles' smallest loops. The only question is, why is Prinzhorn on one side of the desk and the schizophrenics on the other? How do we decide who belongs on which side of the desk?

We lock up people who gravely and harmfully trespass the limits of understanding. We consider harmlessly insane those systems of interpretation which violate the bounds of good sense by consensus, the bounds which separate that which can be understood from that which cannot. Some things have meaning; some things do not. It is well not to confuse the categories.

Why is it sane to find meaning in a doodle and insane to find meaning in a puddle of rain? Why is it sane to count the incidence of the word "murder" in Shakespeare and insane to count frost cracks in the sidewalk? Why is mathematics sane and numerology insane? Why is astronomy sane and astrology insane? Why is it sane to perform an autopsy and insane to read entrails? Why can we sanely inspect the clouds to learn tomorrow's weather, but not the sex of an unborn child? Why is it sane to assign meaning to the elements of a Nepalese altar and insane to assign meaning to the elements in a chemical compound?

The boundaries of sense are actually quite clear. We commonly (if tacitly) agree that the human world has human meaning which we can discover, and the given natural world does not. That human beings and human culture are "natural" phenomena is undeniable;

nevertheless, we draw our intellectual line so it divides the human from the inhuman—quite rightly. We separate culture from nature; we perform a limited set of intellectual operations on natural things and a more extensive set of operations on cultural things. And we agree that it is sane to inquire what cultural things mean and insane to inquire what natural things mean. Doodles, Shakespeare, and Nepalese altars are human; we can interpret their human significance. Puddles, frost cracks, clouds, and chemical compounds are not human and have no human significance. Mathematics, astronomy, and meteorology operate on nature without expecting the objects of their study to bear significant messages to living people. Numerology, astrology, and all forms of divination do; they seek human meaning in raw nature. You may plausibly chart types and meanings of schizophrenic doodle loops; but if you chart types and meanings of clouds and stones, they will come and carry you away. You will have regressed historically; you will have crossed the border, and committed yourself to the other side of the desk.

There are, then, two classes of phenomena on earth: those to which we may reasonably assign human meaning, and those to which we may not. I have I hope established not only that some things have meaning, but also which these are. Now, it is interesting to look at the branches of Western knowledge in the light of this theoretical distinction, in order to assign a slot to criticism, and ultimately to art itself.

Let us take the positivists at their word for the nonce and say that the physical and biological sciences and the other branches of knowledge modeled upon them traffic in data and in purely physical interpretations of data. The object of their study is the raw, unmediated universe. The results are positivist, material, mechanical schemes. Science does not ask what a honeybee means.

The interpretative fields, in contrast, may ask what a sewing bee means. The interpretative fields, which include art and literary criticism, clinical and theoretical psychology, cultural anthropology, sociology of knowledge, comparative religion, theoretical linguistics, and so forth, interpret only things human. They interpret all things human. They produce data, of course, and also interpretations in the abstract realm of human meaning. Nothing human is alien. They may interpret skip-rope rhymes, hospitality etiquette, pottery decoration, slang, warfare, verse drama, skirt length, baby talk, management techniques, nightmares, and economic classifications. Whatever is human may be understood by humans. We may not *exhaust* its meaning; but, again, we may know aught without knowing all.

Science, on the other hand, produces physical interpretations of raw data, of hard data. An objection arises here, for I have already said that *all* knowledge is interpretative and that every scientific datum is an edited abridgment. I must abandon this point temporarily; the positivists usually deny it, and it is well to let them define their own field. And if it is true, it is universal, and therefore useless and niggling. For everyone agrees that some things are more interpretative than others, that a measurement is less interpretative than a piece of literary criticism, and that Mrs. Marx's reading of a thermometer differs in kind from Mr. Marx's reading of history. So let us yield to science, and even rub scientists' faces in it a bit, and say that science, unlike every other human endeavor, is not itself biased, is not culture-blind and bounded.

Here we have science, then, producing data and physical schemes. It studies the raw universe at large and also, statistically, the world of men (demography, behavioral psychology, physical anthropology, etc.). Science studies what we might boisterously call "things as they are." The interpretative fields, on the other hand, and interestingly enough, produce interpretations of interpretations. The bits of human culture they study are already edited selections and humanly meaningful arrangements. When you study Shakespeare or a Nepalese altar or even a schizophrenic doodle, you are studying a human interpretation of things. A language, a philosophy, a religion, a nightmare, a pattern on a pot, and a skip-rope rhyme are human interpretations of things. (So are all forms of science but modern Western science!) The interpretative fields interpret kinds of human order. All interpreters are like critics in this way: they require that someone else has been there first. A person or a culture knits up an artifact, and an interpreter comes along and unravels it.

This division of knowledge is odd. It excludes mathematics and music altogether. It separates the branches of knowledge less by the objects of their study (world or artifact) than by the scope of their results: positivist data and schemes on one hand, and human significance in addition to data on the other. Examining the university curriculum in this light is like examining the physical layout of an asylum. Both the university and the asylum illustrate those boundaries of interpretation which the West has accepted since the Enlightenment: man makes sense; nature does not.

In addition to raising an interesting theoretical question, the examination of which will occupy the rest of this book, this curious division of knowledge may, and quite incidentally, clarify the bitterness of the infighting within so many disciplines, particularly within those many disciplines, like philosophy and the social sciences, which operate on human phenomena. For some workers who prize and seek positivist methods and results must work cheek by jowl with the leaky-minded interpreters. A behaviorist has no truck with Jung, nor a physical anthropologist with Lévi-Strauss, nor a demographer with Marx. A bibliographer who works with a computer all day may find poetry criticism a bit iffy. Yet the ordinary division of knowledge by subject matter—which, after all, is perfectly sensible—means that these disparate kinds of thinkers must share a hall, a batch of student majors, a departmental vote, and a Xerox machine.

(Outside academia, many people have not yet learned of the positivist cast of disciplines like psychology and philosophy. High school seniors and college freshmen tell their advisers that they are interested in "psychology"; it turns out they have read some Jung or Freud. After a semester or two of psychology courses they bail out of the major. Similarly, some students who have read Camus are interested in "philosophy." Many of these students wind up in literature courses, where, they say, they are quite surprised to find, both in the literature and in the critical approaches to it, the interpretative structures and the inquiry into final meanings which they had sought originally and despaired of ever finding in the classroom.)

The theoretical question posed by our division of

knowledge is this: will criticism interpret for us the world at large?

Science will not do it. Will criticism? The interpretative fields handle restricted objects—personality, texts, and so forth. You could not come up with a Freudian reading of celestial mechanics or (I devoutly hope) a Marxist reading of doodles. But criticism in the arts is not so limited. Since art itself interprets both nature and many aspects of culture, art criticism is used to handling a wide variety of objects: personality, landscape, history, ideas, change, the works. Art criticism, then, of all the interpretative disciplines, would seem to be best suited for interpreting the world at large. Literary criticism in particular is well adapted to handling a variety of worldly bits and every degree of abstraction, and to telling us what they mean.

But alas, art criticism works only on art. I had hoped that when the boundaries of art fell, critics would be loosed upon the world; they would interpret the world itself. (This hope was not, I think, widely shared.) But the boundaries of art did not fall; they merely expanded to include the possibility of everything. Criticism has stayed well within its traditional bounds by requiring as usual the intervention of an artist between the object of interpretation and the interpreter. Anything may be art, and so the critic may discuss anything—but only as art.

Octavio Paz's new book of essays raises the issue of Duchamp; Roger Shattuck comments in the *Times* on Duchamp's question: " 'Can one produce works that are not works of art?' He tried; we wouldn't allow it." Whatever any artist produces is subject to art criticism, *and so* has discernible meaning! But it has meaning only as art. When Duchamp exhibits a bottle rack, criticism can interpret the bottle rack only as art object; criticism must remain dumb on the significance of bottle racks in toto. When Capote and Mailer call their factual accounts novels, criticism may interpret their materials in the light of art; criticism may interpret the authors' interpretation of events; but sadly, criticism cannot tell us the meaning, *sub specie aeternitatis,* of the Clutter murders or the life and death of Gary Gilmore.

Critics, then, interpret neither the natural world nor the cultural world directly. Critics can discuss a whale or a bottle rack only if Melville or a Duchamp has already selected and stilled those objects and shaped them for the mind. All this is, I'm afraid, self-evident to almost everyone but a very few people, to whom it comes as a continuous shock and disappointment.

Can we not loose the methods of literary criticism upon the raw world? May we not analyze the breadth of our experience? We can and may—but only if we first consider the raw world as a text, as a meaningful, purposefully fashioned creation, as a work of art. For we have seen that critics interpret artifacts only. Our interpreting the universe as an artifact absolutely requires that we posit an author for it, or a celestial filmmaker, dramatist, painter, sculptor, composer, architect, or choreographer.* And no one has been willing openly to posit such an artist for the universe since the American transcendentalists and before them the Medieval European philosophers.

---

* This, clearly, would be a religious, even creationist, reading of the universe. Note how it differs from pantheism. It reads the universe as a significant art object, not as part of a stream of being which includes the observer, and not as personal message. Pantheism is not the only meaningful reading of the natural world. One need not find a spirit in each bush and rock for these things to mean. The bush and rock may be, as it were, literary symbols. But of what? If we could only see the first draft, or locate some letters!

CHAPTER 9

Can Fiction Interpret
the World?

We are missing a whole class of investigators: those who interpret the raw universe in terms of meaning. If science will not seek human meaning, and if interpreters (critics, anthropologists, etc.) study human events and human artifacts only, then who will tell us the meaning of the raw universe? By the raw universe I mean here all that we experience, all things cultural and natural, all of the universe that is known, given, made, and changing: the world, and they that dwell therein. Experience is something human, even our experience of dumb nature. It is sane to seek to understand it in all its breadth. Breadth is, after all, characteristic of our experience. If we confine our interpretative investigations to strictly bounded aspects of culture, like skip-rope rhymes or the

Battle of Manassas, we miss learning what we most want to know.

Who is doing this? Who interprets the raw world directly? Schizophrenics do this, and superstitious people, and pantheists, all in their several fashions. Following a tradition at least as old as Aristotle, some scientists of our time interpret limited sets of data in terms of human meaning (B. F. Skinner, Edmund O. Wilson). Who else? Prophets and the founders of religions interpret the broad world directly. Theologians and metaphysical philosophers, if there are any, do. And artists do.

We mistrust schizophrenics, pantheists, and superstitious people. Science's interpreters (those who are not drawn like Lewis Thomas and Richard Selzer into the welcoming arms of literature) are apt to be innocent outside their fields (Jaynes) or, worse, so steeped in positivism (Wilson, Skinner) that they try to make a virtue of ignorance by denying that anything else exists. The findings of former religious investigations repel some people, and new prophets and leaders arise but rarely; when they do, they speak the same hard words. We have a shortage of metaphysicians. This leaves artists.

Individual artists are unlikely to produce interpretations of experience so broad and valuable as those of, say, Moses, Buddha, Plato, Paul, or Kant. Nevertheless, artists are almost the sole contemporary workers in the field. And since paint, wood, steel, motion, and musical tones do not necessarily refer to any particular aspects of the world, and since words do indeed refer to all the aspects of the world that we know—nature, culture, feeling, and idea—the literary arts are in a better position to interpret the world in all its breadth than are the other arts.

I am certainly not going to insist upon this curiously central position of the arts, and especially the literary arts, in relation to all knowledge. If I actually believed that the progress of human understanding depended on our crop of contemporary novelists, I would shoot myself. We have not lost all that has already been written, nor have we yet understood it. It is merely very interesting to consider literature this way: as a formal assignment of meaning to many things, as a kind of interpretative criticism with the great world as its object. This view sheds a curious, even weird, light on fiction, and also, incidentally, on poetry.

For lyric poetry, of all the arts—of all human endeavor—does this very thing, first and best. Throughout its long history all over the world, lyric poetry has been less fanciful than fiction. A book of lyric poems is most often a collation of interpreted facts. Poetry's materials, its characters, objects, and events, its landscapes and cities, its mornings and afternoons, are far more likely to have been actual than fabricated. This means that poetry has been able to function quite directly as human interpretation of the raw, loose universe. It is a mixture, if you will, of journalism and metaphysics, or of science and religion.

So we are all the more disappointed when poets shirk, when they bait their hooks with tidbits and fish for small fry in their backyards. Very often poets limit their take of the actual to wee private moments the significance of which they assert on only personal grounds. It is a shame that poetry has decayed to such sensory self-indulgence that it has abdicated that task to which it is so well and uniquely suited.

How a Whale Means

Where does this leave fiction? We must grant from the ✓
start that to hope that fiction can do a sober and useful
job of interpreting the universe is preposterous. It is preposterous on many grounds. For one thing, fiction, especially Old World fiction, is scarcely concerned with any
materials but cultural ones—with only the odd moor or
mountain thrown in for scenery. So even if fiction does
interpret, it interprets the human arena almost solely.
And its results differ from those of more limited and rig-
orous interpretative fields like history and moral philosophy mainly in their sloppiness, insouciance, and inac-
cessibility.

For another thing, we may question whether any art,
let alone fiction, is especially interpretative at all. Of
course, insofar as fiction writers select materials from the
world, they interpret them, for every selection is an interpretation. But this is no great distinction, for *all* mental
activity is selective and interpretative; all language is interpretative; all perception is interpretative; all expression
and activity is interpretative. And all interpretations miss
their mark or invent it, make it up. Humanity has but
one product, and that is fiction. On this head, fiction is
no more interpretative than any other mental product
such as eyesight or gossip. It is merely more fictive. It is,
in fact, by definition a tissue of lies.

Fiction is fabrication. Fabrication is itself, of course, an ✓
ordering or rearrangement of selected materials from the
actual world. But fiction's resemblance to, say, botany
stops here. Every fiction writer knows that he selects materials and fabricates unsystematically, according to love,
whim, and convenience. The fiction writer is astonished

to note that some materials fit a particular idea for order so well that he finds himself writing whole books about peripheral or random objects to which he has never previously devoted a care or a thought (which may account for the quality of much that we read). He will grant at once, abashed, that his work's ordering structure does not necessarily derive from the materials themselves, but derives instead from bright ideas in the middle of the night, tabloid newspapers, misunderstood snippets of small talk or philosophy, dreams, outlandish coincidences, jokes, and other sources so suspect and dubious he blushes to name them. When a writer actually "selects" his materials, he chooses them to fit. This process violates every principle which legitimate, responsible interpreters use in order to approach a limited object with a minimum of prejudice. A writer obtains his materials, and his ideas of order, by the arbitrary and unscrupulous processes of eruption on one hand and plunder on the other.

Art is a terrible interpreter. The artist's intention is not to learn what exists but to create what never before existed. He wishes to make an interesting art object. Art cares not if it truly knows the world. Art prizes originality more than fidelity. This preference drives it to consider trivial bits of world whose possible significance is of little moment, or to handle momentous materials in flashy and dishonest ways.

Worse still, and damnably in this setting, art's interpretations take the form of contexts. They may not apply at all to the great world outside the artistic context. Melville assigned to whiteness, to a doubloon, and to a whale a great load of significance in *Moby-Dick*; but who could say that, since Melville, we as a race have a greater understanding than we ever did of the human significance of whiteness, doubloons, or whales? It would be better to say that Melville interprets the world through the *agency* of *Moby-Dick* and its parts, and that the whale is the tool of interpretation and not its object; but even so, what can we say of Melville's interpretation of the world in *Moby-Dick* apart from *Moby-Dick*—apart from the context of the art object itself? Can we say anything? How, then, may we regard *Moby-Dick* or any other art object as interpretative?

I think we must conclude, under pressure from the arguments above, that fiction per se is not interpretation per se. A novel is not a critical analysis.

But—and this is a fine distinction—a work of fiction is indeed *interpretative* in the special sense that it is, by intention, an object to be interpreted. Unlike the critic, who intends his interpretation to be near the level of a "final say," and who does not, at any rate, expect the world to devote much energy to analyzing his interpretation, the fiction writer intends his work to be a primary object. He intends it to be interpreted. This is the sense in which we can say that fiction is interpretative. It applies to all fiction; it applies especially clearly to traditional fiction which intends to present a picture of the actual world.

People interpret the world, undeniably, and a fiction writer like Mann on one hand and Borges on the other may deliberately produce a work of fiction to delineate and objectify his interpretation. He will fashion a miniature world whose parts are selected and ordered in such a way that no one examining them could fail to interpret them more or less as he does. We may perhaps gingerly infer that the writer himself interprets the actual world along the same lines as those we interpret out of his created world—though such an inference is both unwarranted and irrelevant. Our inquiring into a writer's personal opinions and private vision of things is bankrupt intellectually and nasty as well. Nevertheless, those opinions and that vision are not entirely irrelevant to the production of the work, unless the writer is an outright hack.

The writer—to continue *pro hominem*—is the world's ✓ interpreter. The writer is certainly interested in the art of fiction, but perhaps less so than the critic is. The critic is interested in the novel; the novelist is interested in his neighbors. Perhaps even more than in his own techniques, then, the writer is interested in knowing the world in order to make real and honest sense of it. He worries the world and probes it; he collects the world and collates it. No part of it is outside his field. All the great world is his field. That is, the novel's potential field is the whole world; any given novel's actual field is only a small wedge of it. But that wedge may include anything: philology, genocide, childbirth, naval architecture, microphysics, love, the dressing of game. The writer is interested in everything (which is why he is such good company)—in hockey and horseshoe crabs and baton twirling. His interest, I think, is genuine. It is not only that he plans to *use* these bits of world in his work; it is actually and wonderfully that he plans to learn them all, for starters, and then to understand them.

For his interpretations of the world to be as valuable and accurate as possible, they must include as much breadth and variety as possible. The aim of the interpretative, referential writer is to render as much of the world as he possibly can as coherent as he possibly can. To this end the writer studies the great world closely, and takes notes. The writer, then, approaches the world exactly as a critic approaches a text.

Instead of a critical analysis of the great world, or of any given wedge of it, the writer produces a simulacrum of it. The work of fiction is a smaller and more coherent world alongside the great world. We may inquire of the world within the work of art all that we inquire of the great world: what, pray, is going on here? What sort of a world is this? Do social matters dominate it, or spiritual matters? Is man himself glorious or shameful? In other words, we can examine an artistic world not only formally, but also culturally, morally, and metaphysically, to gain insight about the great world—the great world that is the truest object of our most urgent inquiries and deepest hopes.

To return to my starting point, then, fiction is not so much itself an interpretation (except insofar as everything is) as it is an object for future interpretation. It is, God help us, a text. Sadly, as an interpretation it is dumb until someone interprets it. The writer "conceals," as it were, his interpretation inside literary materials which feign lifelikeness on one hand or elaborately wrought surfaces on the other. The lifelike materials absorb us and draw us into the narrative; the wrought surfaces suspend us over a semi-opaque surface of words and images. One feints, the other dazzles. Each of these kinds of fictional handling has, as a secondary property, the effect of misleading us, the readers; both of them lure us to drink from Lethe, whose soothing waters make us forget that the whole show is only a subterfuge by means of which some loquacious and probably half-educated crank is making us sit still and listen to his theories.

In Zola novels, for instance, we might find in the sum of particular cases the generalization that an individual's place in the mechanism of society determines his fate. In *Moby-Dick*, however, we might discover a different reading of the world at large: an individual's fate is determined not so much by his society as by his own private character. In the controlled world of the novel, these things are optional. A gifted writer can make almost any option work, almost any opinion stick—especially as we seldom read fiction for its interpretations in the first place. The reduction of literary works to pious epigrams is a jolly parlor game and little more. Nevertheless, such generalized relationships, truisms or not, are yours for the asking in any fiction, and they may be of major importance (at least to the writer, who has to start somewhere) as the principles upon which the work is founded. Contemporary modernist fiction is no exception. From any work of fiction we may derive an interpretative view of the world.

Of course, the novel, even the unabashed novel of ideas, is not a tract. Insofar as it is complex and honest, it will be enriched by a certain amount of contradiction which gives depth and rondure to ideas; insofar as it is energetic and powerful, it will have the vigor of many clashing materials; insofar as it is broad and broken, like the great world, much that is in it will make little or no sense.

Unless we are Marxists or fundamentalists, we do not judge a literary work according to whether or not we agree with its world view. Nor do we usually devote critical attention to its views on their own merits apart from the work. Nevertheless, when the interpretations are absolutely stupid, we shun the work no matter how strong its surface. When the fictional world is contrived to point up some miserable cliché, such as that man is threatening his own habitat, we dismiss the work. Yet when the fictional world is contrived to point up some interesting interpretative relationship, we will read it— even sometimes if its writing is clumsy (*A Voyage to Arcturus, The Diary of a Country Priest*). This is as it should be.

Complexity, subtlety, and breadth are the virtues here. If a writer is going to engage in the intellectual business of assigning meanings and showing relationships, he had better think very well. The novel of ideas had better be good. We are not interested in simple allegory, nor in a world so biased as to be unrecognizable, nor in any excited shoutings about. For most of us, the "whole truth" is necessarily complex; to simplify is to fudge. Nobody wants to read a well-ground axe.

On the other hand, a novel is not a kind of very long-playing but lightweight television set. We are no longer children, and we no longer enjoy fiction with our eyes only. We seek, as I say, a complex, subtle, and broad set of ideas. But in our horror of oversimplification and piety we may have bent too far in the other direction. We are so accustomed to finding intelligent ideas and excellent surfaces together, and stupid ideas and clumsy surfaces together, that in our decadence or in our haste we may fail to inquire beyond appearances. As a result, we undoubtedly miss some interesting thinking. And—importantly—writers who have only an ear for prose and a taste for subtle surfaces may be credited with having a good deal more. We may actually assume such writers have something on their minds. We may even ascribe to them a thought-out interpretation of the world, which we may then seek in their works. It may be this factor more than any other which leads to the common assertion that the theme of twentieth-century fiction is meaninglessness. Meaninglessness, that is, may actually be not so much a deliberate theme as it is an inadvertent achievement.

Find the Hidden Meaning

Fiction elicits an interpretation of the world by being itself a worldlike object for interpretation. It is a subtle pedagogy. When the thoughtful reader or critic interprets the work as text (and only then), when he inquires into the work's structures and assumptions, he will be led to formulate a set of relationships obtaining in the work which will correspond (since words refer) to a limited and exaggerated interpretation of experience itself. Sadly, the interpretative aspects of fiction absolutely require further interpretation by a reader in order to exist. They are simply not present to the senses, but rather concealed behind materials, until they are interpreted out. If you really have "something to say" in literary fiction, then, you will have to interest a critic in your work, or somehow interest your readers in analyzing its structure—or else what you "have to say" will go unheard. For this reason, it is a pity that so few critics work on contemporary fiction.

All this is a paradoxical situation for intellectuals who turn to fiction as the best possible prose vehicle for their interpretations, only to discover that those very interpretations—the urgency of which prompted the work—are to the reader the work's most dispensable aspect. They discover that in order to write fiction that anybody might want to read, they must painstakingly conceal what is to them its very point. (Here is the germ of truth in that funny, sweet saying of the ignorant, that the function of criticism in general, and of freshman critical essays in particular, is to "find the hidden meaning.") In order to make a world in which their ideas might be discovered, writers embody those ideas in materials solid and opaque, and thus conceal them. In the process of fleshing out a thought, they brick it in. The more subtle they are as artists (not as thinkers, but as artists), the more completely their structures will vanish into the work, and the more grouchy they will become the more readers tell them what lovely, solid bricks they make.

Insofar as a writer is interested in interpretation, then, he is stuck in this paradox. His role is like that of a scout whose job it is to blaze a new trail, all traces of which he must carefully obliterate. When the writer completely covers his traces, he is no longer said to be writing the novel of ideas.

If the novel of ideas constitutes a kind of *via positiva*, a fiction of openness, of bold and faithful action in which the writer permits his understanding of things to be bared, its complement, the fiction of aestheticism, is a kind of *via negativa* in which the writer (Chekhov, Flaubert) finds himself by losing himself.

In such fiction, ideas dissolve into their materials without a trace. This is the very opposite of contemporary modernist fiction. In contemporary modernist works (in *Pale Fire* or *Ficciones*), the relationships among bare ideas constitute the real action. Narrative materials are a thin tattooed skin flattened over the structural bones. These works are as purely intellectual as art can contrive. But the apparently motiveless fiction of which I speak is as purely material as art can contrive. In *Dubliners*, in *Madame Bovary*, in Chekhov stories, materials stand purified of their causes. Each narrative event is a material object, a mute given, as shorn of apparent cause and idea as any tree. This is an art of perfect concealment. And it illustrates the writer's paradox very well.

Take the Bellow story "Leaving the Yellow House." Bellow has covered his tracks even more thoroughly (if less tensely) than Joyce did in "The Dead." You may read this story half a dozen times before you discover, by prolonged and even extraordinary inquiry into its title, that it is not about survival, as it appears to be, but about dying, and the relationship between soul and body, the loaning of matter to spirit for a time. The vivid character and her elaborated setting are actually designed to be as minimal as possible. Bellow describes, in specifics which lend her supreme importance, an old woman living alone at Sego Lake Desert, Utah. The surface of the story is full of interesting action; the life at hand, however, is specifically as reduced and empty as imagination permits. This enormous, unstated metaphor gives Bellow a chance to examine what we have when we have only life itself, when we have as our sole possession only a yellow house—only a living body—which we must leave. (This is not criticism, note, but blithe assertion.) Now, there is not one blessed clue in the body of the text to these considerations I have just sketched. Yet if you read the story you will see that all its materials fall under this head and no other. As a reader, however, you may easily omit to worry about any of this. The story lacks nothing; it needs no excuse; it raises no questions about its principles. You may enjoy the story alone, or in the light of character and survival; or you may enjoy the story in the light of its actual sense. (I trust you did not greatly enjoy my account of the sense alone.) The sense is optional; it is dispensable. And you will not absorb it from the story as it were subliminally; you must seek it out and articulate it, or do without.

What are we to make of this silly state of affairs called art, that a writer should go to all the trouble to say something interesting so well that scarcely anyone will ever hear it? How wonderful, people say, that we may read a good work on so many different levels! What they do not go on to say is how seldom they bother, and in fact, how much bother it is, to poke and poke at something which you are enjoying anyway. But, dammit, is a work of art really about what it is about, or is it not? My bias here is plain.

The interpretative, referential structures by which writers make sense of the world occupy an unenviable position: they fascinate or obsess the writer and escape or bore the reader. The reader enjoys his books like so many skinless sausages dropped on his plate.

And what does this mean? Is a book's interpretative structure merely the harmless hobby of the writer and a few critics? To what extent does a work's intellectual structure contribute to its value?

One school of thought holds that a work's greatest value coincides with its greatest appeal; that literature is a joy and not a puzzle, essay, or lecture; that readers quite reasonably like what they like, not what some critic thinks they should like; that writers know not what they really do, because the final value and significance of a writer's work lies in whatever shiny materials happen to attract a casual reader's eye; and that "Leaving the Yellow House" (by this account) is a fascinating depiction of aging, or a great character study, or a colorful and desolate depiction of Utah, or of life in any American small town.

Another view, which is both more respectable and even more discouraging, grants that a work's interpretative and intellectual structures have value, but only a practical one. They serve the writer, and the writer alone. They serve him either as motive or as scaffolding. As motive they get him out of bed in the morning. They interest him sufficiently in the work that he will begin it and see it through. As scaffolding they serve the writer as abstract superstructures. They are organizing principles which are utterly vital to the process of construction and utterly obsolete when the job is done. As scaffolding, then, they merely give the writer a place to stand in order to lay his bricks.

This is a miserable problem, but it is not a problem for all fiction writers. This is a good century for writers like the contemporary modernists who wish to make their works' aesthetic structures plainly visible; all the arts have moved in this direction. Writers whose vision is almost wholly formalized, and not referential or interpretative, have free rein. And writers who are sitting on a story absolutely great in its own right have no problem either; if they have little extra to say, they also have little to hide. The paradox hurts only frankly interpretative thinkers, who have a theory or two about the world, as well as an art; their sort of thinking is frowned upon in fiction. Such a writer has several options. He may pursue his own bent, either hoping to effect, single-handedly, a change in our taste in fiction, or hoping more modestly that our taste will change of its own accord sooner or later. He may then, like Thomas Mann or Aldous Huxley (or like Shaw in drama), toss it all in, right there in cold, discursive type, or with the flimsiest veneer of narrative artifice, and risk being thought the clumsier storyteller for it. His hope in this case is that the work's other virtues will outweigh this particular vice, or that its other virtues will at least get it read. If he persists in making plain his thoughts, his only other hope is for a name as ringing as "Thomas Mann"; such an institutionalized set of syllables licenses anything. Alternately, he gives up; he yields. Still wishing to be heard, he nevertheless perfects his aesthetic surface, obliterates his tracks, dismantles his scaffolding, and prays or weeps silently under his pile of bricks. His only hope, then, is that his story will have such enormous appeal that some critic will take it to the beach.

In most cases, the writer of thoughtful literary fiction chooses the second route, but simply cannot refrain from waving little flags from his hiding place under the bricks. He makes liberal use of epigraphs which plainly raise the intellectual issues at hand. He gives his work a mystifying title. He names his characters "Mrs. Graal" or "Zooey" or variations on, or anagrams of, Zeus, Christ, Beelzebub, Plato, or Darwin. He slips other clues into the text, either with a syringe or with a sledgehammer: he will unexpectedly liken an infectious disease to human immorality, or Cro-Magnon man to a nuclear physicist.

It is demeaning that serious novelists have to resort to such coyness. But interpretative fiction is very much out of fashion. There are, however, two ameliorating circumstances. One is that the fictional surface may embody its idea so beautifully well that the writer may, if he wishes, spell it out without forcing or pleading. Always, if the work is good enough, the writer can get away with anything. Thus at the end of "The Dead," Joyce may do with us what he will; he may even tell us a little bit about what has been going on.

The other ameliorating circumstance is more subtle; I am not sure that it even exists. It could be, however, that aesthetic perfection in a work of fiction carries with it a certain felt tension of tone which not only awes the reader, so that he judges the work to be absolutely excellent, but also inspires him to consider it deeply. It is "The Dead," again, which leads me to this thought. Its perfection is of the purely aesthetic kind—which is perhaps the only kind of perfection possible for fiction (we do not speak of "perfection" in Mann, Melville, Conrad, Dostoevsky, or even Shakespeare, but of other values instead). The perfection of "The Dead" resides in the total disappearance of ideas into their materials. Why this? we ask, as we ask of the great world: Why this, and not some other?

The story contains no trace of that bundle of bias, enthusiasm, motive, morality, personality, and mind which we might term "the author." Where is Joyce? The work is seamless. I do not mean that Joyce does not intrude his opinions into his story—that is a pleasing but not uncommon virtue—but instead I mean something more profound and less easy to name. The sentences have in their rhythms an austerity that is complete. They exhibit, by their perfect concealment of it, an absolutely controlled tension, like that of a mastered grief or longing. I suggest that the austerity with which a writer wholly subsumes his thoughts to his fictional materials reminds us of—or is even identical to—the difficult dignity with which some people control strong and private feelings. We are people, and we call this "power"; it will always command our respect.

Perhaps, then, this high degree of tension and control in prose, this sense of great emotional passion at short rein, attracts our mind and leads us to inquire into the sources of the tension and the principles of control. And perhaps, too, the absence of any hint of explanation or motive on the author's part will lead us to seek it, lead us to inquire, as we do of "Leaving the Yellow House" and, somewhat differently, of "The Dead," what these things are doing here in the first place. I hope so.

CHAPTER 10

About Symbol, and with a Diatribe Against Purity

Fiction does interpret the world at large. It traffics in understanding. Does it also traffic in knowledge? Do its interpretations have the status of hard data? Does art know?

Knowledge and understanding meet where science meets theology, where substance and idea mingle their parts. This juncture is the apex of the pyramid of abstractions. It is the apogee of all our researches; it is the vanishing point where all lines of thought converge. Here eternity gives birth to time. I wish to assert that art is especially competent to penetrate these regions, and others as well.

Zola, according to Charles Child Walcutt, said that fiction "had been an art but would henceforth be an instru-ment for the scientific study of man and society." Now, no one is going to attack Zola, who is not so much a sacred cow as a dead horse. Let me just use these notions. Zola makes a false distinction when he says that fiction was formerly an art but was now an instrument for scientific study—an instrument, I infer, like a lens or a sextant. Because the truth is that only by being art is fiction an instrument at all. Art itself is an instrument, a cognitive instrument, and with religion the only instrument, for probing certain materials and questions. Art and religion probe the mysteries in those difficult areas where blurred and powerful symbols are the only possible speech and their arrangement into coherent religions and works of art the only possible grammar.

All art may be said to be symbolic in this sense: it is a material mock-up of bright idea. Any work of art symbolizes the process by which spirit generates matter, or materials generate idea. Any work of art symbolizes juncture itself, the socketing of eternity into time and energy into form. Of course, all that man makes is similar in this respect: a bowl, a highway, and a triangle are also material mock-ups of mental orders. But this is *all* that art is, in essence and by intent. A highway intends something quite other. Any art object is essentially a model in which the creative process is frozen with its product in its arms.

Any art object as a whole is symbolic, then. But more pertinent to my point is the familiar level at which an art object is symbolic because its parts are. These things warrant a brief restatement.

An allegorical symbol is precise and bounded. When fair-haired Virtue shatters the opium pipe of Indolence, we may conclude that moral virtue in the abstract, which the author finds as attractive as he finds blondes, rejects indolence, strongly. Nonallegorical symbols, which are the topic at hand, are not precise. It is when these symbols break their allegorical boundaries, their commitment to reference, that they start stepping out on us. The laxity of their bonds permits them to enter unsuspected relationships. They become suggestive. These artistic symbols do not represent things in the great world directly, as the opium pipe represents indolence. Instead, these symbols, like art objects themselves, are semi-enclosed worlds of meaning the essence of whose referential substance we may approximate, but whose boundaries and total possibilities for significance we can never locate precisely or exhaust.

Of the "stately pleasure dome" of "Kubla Khan," shall we say it is an ordered, pleasing, and aloof work of art ("A stately pleasure dome"); or any conscious product of active power ("decree"); or the passive receptacle of the wellspring of the creative imagination itself ("Where Alph, the sacred river, ran"); or a formal ordering of subconscious materials ("Through caverns measureless to man"); or the civilization from which instruments of cognition are launched which discover and illuminate that civilization's sources in chaos, or its fated destiny, or its brute environment ("Down to a sunless sea")? Of course, these are just opening suggestions; the other parts of the poem shed much light on the pleasure dome, clarifying some interpretations and suggesting others. Complete readings of the poem are available. If we even begin to investigate "Kubla Khan," do we not hazard into realms where paraphrase is inadequate? Of course. That is truism. Well, then, does this not mean that the pleasure dome and other symbolic parts of the poem, and the poem itself, are vehicles of understanding? They are not the express products of past knowledge and understanding, such as the expression $2 + 3 = 5$, or the statement that virtue rejects indolence; instead, they are new objects wherein new understanding may be sought and found. They are objects set beyond the limits of the already known.

We may find symbolized in "Kubla Khan"—by the dome, by Kubla Khan, the river and its fountain, the forests, the caverns, the sea, the ice, and the Abyssinian maid and her song—something of the relationship between order and chaos, and between spirit and matter, between the artist and his materials, and the artist and society ("Ancestral voices prophesying war!"), and the romantic imagination and its sources and values ("A savage place! as holy and enchanted"), and the dangerously close relationship in the art object and perhaps in the artist between inspirational sources and the appalling chaos of the abyss ("the mingled measure/From the fountain and the caves"). We are interested in these relationships. The poem presents them. The poem is a form of knowledge.*

But what is knowledge if we cannot state it? If art objects quit the bounds of the known and make blurry feints at the unknown, can they truly add to knowledge or understanding? I think they can; for although we may never exhaust or locate precisely the phenomena they signify, we may nevertheless approximate them—and

* Incidentally, "Kubla Khan" also raises the question of its own beauty. Why is it so beautiful? Why do otherwise rational people—sober, grouchy, skeptical people—turn soft in the head about "Kubla Khan"? Why is this creepy-crawly, misty, overlandscaped, striving-after-beautiful-effect, watercolorish little portentous poem one of the most beautiful and powerful poems in English?

this, of course, is our position in relation to all knowledge and understanding. All our knowledge is partial and approximate; if we are to know electrons and chimpanzees less than perfectly, and call it good enough, we may as well understand phenomena like love and death, or art and freedom, imperfectly also.

Artistic symbol, in other words, instead of merely imitating the flux and mystery of the great world, actually penetrates them on its own. That is, if a document like *The New York Times* or Pepys' *Diary* is a kind of island miniature of our planet, an island which we may explore on foot, then a symbol or a structure of related symbols (including myth, religion, and innumerable works of art, like *Moby-Dick* and "Kubla Khan") is, by contrast, a kind of exploratory craft. It is a space probe. Although it is constructed of the planet's materials, it nevertheless leaves the planet altogether. It is a rocket ship; it opens new and hitherto inaccessible regions.

This is the unique cognitive property of symbol: there is no boundary, and probably no difference, between symbol and the realm it comes to mean. An art object, say, and a myth are each the agent and the object of cognition. Each is a lens focused on itself. Say that the story of Christ is a symbol. Say that generations of thinkers have enlarged and enriched the symbol. What then? What is the difference between this narrative, or this artifact, and what it symbolizes? It is it, itself. You cannot address this question (or any other) in depth without using its own terms, which are symbolic at every level: cup, manger, and cross, or grace, incarnation, and sacrifice—and so on, either "up" or "down" the levels of abstraction. You must either learn to use these terms, and like them, or relinquish this field of knowledge altogether.

Similarly, to speak of "Kubla Khan" at any useful level is to speak of the pleasure dome and of Alph the sacred river, and the caverns measureless to man, and the Abyssinian maid. You learn the poem as you learn Italian. You cease to translate its bits in your mind, and instead let them speak for themselves. All our knowledge is of course in one sense symbolic, and to go deeply into any field—physics, say, or art—is to learn faith in its symbols. At first you notice that these tools and objects of thought are symbols; you translate them, as you go, into your own familiar idiom. Later you learn faith and release them. You learn to let them relate on their own terms, hadron to hadron, paint surface to paint surface—and only then do you begin to make progress. (In this sense, faith is the requisite of knowledge.)

One interesting, well-known, yet elusive thing about true symbols is something unmanageable about the way they are formed. Since their regions of meaning are blurred, and since there is no clear difference between symbols and the realms they come to mean, and since they act at the level where the scarcely understood fades into the unknown, the hapless artist who sets one of these things in motion shortly finds himself out of control. Symbols, and the many works of art that contain them, "assume a life of their own," as the cliché goes; they outreach the span of their maker's arm; they guide their creator's hand; they illuminate a wider area than that which their maker ever intended. I will show, shortly, that the art object is always passive in relation to its audience. It is alarmingly active, however, in relation to its creator. Far from being like a receptacle in which you, the artist, drop your ideas, and far from being like a lump of clay which you pummel until it fits your notion of an ashtray, the art object is more like an enthusiastic and ill-trained Labrador retriever which yanks you into traffic. I do not intend to wax mystical or sentimental at this juncture; nevertheless, this familiar notion—that the art object drags its maker into deep waters—is worth mentioning again, matter-of-factly, as one evidence that art, especially insofar as it is symbolic art, is not only an object of past knowledge but an instrument of new knowledge. For if you already understood all the relationships among phenomena to which the parts of your art referred, you could control them easily from the start—and you cannot. It is the artist's business, then, to learn from his art and to order formally his new understanding. Confused art is merely confusing. When in the art object the artist has mastered his own confusion, he has gained new ground; and if he is mature enough and educated enough to have begun at the far edge of his own culture's knowledge, then he has won new ground not only for himself but for his culture as well.

Symbol does not only refer; it acts. There is no such thing as a *mere* symbol. When you climb to the higher levels of abstraction, symbols, those enormous, translucent planets, are all there is. They are at once your only tools of knowledge and that knowledge's only object. It is no leap to say that space-time is itself a symbol. If the material world is a symbol, it is the symbol of mind, or of God. Which is more or less meaningless—as you choose. But it is not *mere*. In the last analysis, symbols and art objects do not stand for things; they manifest them, in their fullness. You begin by using symbols, and end by contemplating them.

A Diatribe Against Purity

As symbol, or as the structuring of symbols, art can render intelligible—or at least visible, at least discussible—those wilderness regions which philosophy has abandoned and those hazardous terrains which science's tools do not fit. I mean the rim of knowledge where language falters; and I mean all those areas of human experience, feeling, and thought about which we care so much and know so little: the meaning of all that we see before us, of our love for each other, and the forms of freedom in time, and power, and destiny, and all whereof we imagine: grace, perfection, beauty, and the passage of all materials to thoughts and of all ideas to forms.

The task, then, of all the arts in each century is to rescue the clichés, not to turn from them, and to dedicate themselves each new decade to more comprehensive forms of beauty and understanding. It is to expand those arts' purviews, to expand the arc of the comprehended world, and not to restrict any vision according to the demands for purity set by theory. Purity of practice guarantees that the artist will not err, and that superficial critics will find no flaw in the work, and that nothing has been ventured. Within the bare pantry of purity, stocked solely with what the mind knows to be essential, symbol, which is itself material and which requires a chaotic wealth of materials, can neither grow nor flourish. Symbols arise from material messes.

Purity is one of the two most attractive ideas the human race knows. The other is perfection. Purity is absence; perfection is fullness. Purity seeks to eliminate; its worshipers from the right or the left wage war with swords. As an idea, purity has been steadily diluting lyric poetry since Valéry. It has wreaked outright havoc in the plastic arts. (In Guillaume Apollinaire's 1913 Cubist manifesto, which runs nine pages, the word "pure" and its variants occurs seventeen times, each time honorifically. "Too many painters," Apollinaire said ominously in the same essay, "still adore plants, stones, the sea, or men." To be pure means to stop all this needless adoration.)

Purity seeks to eliminate inessentials. But even if we could agree on the essentials of any art (which we patently cannot), what have we got when we are "down" to them? It is hard to see how anyone could think, even in the abstract, that a purging of inessentials is good in itself. Who would want to see the woods purified of inessentials? His children? By the time the arts are down to their various irreducible nubs, they dissolve into concepts; they lose the material energy which made them interesting.

When the art object contains a wealth of varied materials, it can act. The coherent relationships among those materials serve as a kind of rocket fuel, so to speak, which propels the object into the regions it explores. But when the object is only a theoretical mock-up of those regions—when it presents only those relationships whose structures are already known—then nothing of the universe can be learned. In the latter sort of object—in the Mondrian—we can study the mind's own structures, and the structures of disembodied relationships, and this is something; but if we really believe that there is a world external to mind, and if it can be known and art can know it, then our ambitions for art are higher. Material complexity is the truth of the world, even the workable world of idea, and must be the truth of the art object which would imitate, order, and penetrate that world: complexity, and contradiction, and repetition, diversity, energy, and largesse. I am as attracted to purity as the next guy. But it must not happen here.

CHAPTER 11

Does the World Have Meaning?

The most extreme, cheerful, and fantastic view of art to which I ever subscribe is one in which the art object requires no viewer or listener—no audience whatever—in order to do what it does, which is nothing less than to hold up the universe.

This is a fundamentally insane notion, which developed in my own mind from an idea of Buckminster Fuller's. Every so often I try to encourage other writers by telling them this cheerful set of thoughts; always they gaze at me absolutely appalled. Fuller's assertion was roughly to this effect: the purpose of people on earth is to counteract the tide of entropy described in the Second Law of Thermodynamics. Physical things are falling apart at a terrific rate; people, on the other hand, put things together. People build bridges and cities and roads; they write music and novels and constitutions; they have ideas. That is why people are here; the universe as it were *needs* somebody or something to keep it from falling apart.

Now, for a long time I have taken this notion of Fuller's to mean something even he probably did not intend: that imaginative acts actually weigh in the balance of physical processes. Imaginative acts—even purely mental combinations, like the thought that a certain cloud resembles a top hat—carry real weight in the universe. A child who makes a pun, or a shepherd who looks at a batch of stars and thinks, "That part is a throne and that part is a swan," is doing something which counts in the universe's reckoning of order and decay—which counts just as those mighty explosions and strippings of electrons do inside those selfsame stars.

This jolly view soothes the Puritan conscience; it gives the artist real work. With his thumb in the dike he is saving the universe. And the best part of it is he need not find a publisher, or a gallery, or a producer, or a symphony orchestra. Thoughts count. A completed novel in a trunk in the attic is an order added to the sum of the universe's order. It remakes its share of undoing. It counteracts the decaying of systems, the breakdown of stars and cultures and molecules, the fraying of forms. It works. (If an essentially mental order and an essentially physical one are equivalents, then all we need are the conversion tables. With a little tinkering, Einstein's formula might work for this. Perhaps a decent line in a decent sonnet weighs in the balance with a bonfire, say, or the force of a very high tide. Could a complex and ordered novel pull the stars from their courses?)

Having disburdened myself of this crackpot notion, a little ghosty story I never tire of telling myself, I shall retreat to firmer ground. All the other interesting views of art require that the art object attract an audience, if only an audience of one.

In this century, orthodoxy no longer believes that art objects act directly upon that audience, by informing its members, for instance, that prison conditions are terrible, or that land use requires management. Whatever the art object does, it does not do it *to* us, actively, like a headmaster with his cane. It is our object, after all; we are not its people. The art object does not teach, exhort, arouse, aid, and so forth. It does not "help us to see" like an optometrist; it does not "make us realize" like a therapist; it does not "open doors for us" like a butler. Nevertheless, insofar as art has any function whatsoever (and I am coming to believe that it does), it requires an audience. It requires an audience just as the tree falling in the forest does; it requires an audience as subject, so that it may be object. If outside human perception the art object has no human value, then the art object needs a perceiver, lest all it is or does be lost.

The art object is always passive in relation to its perceiver. A book which no one is reading rests in its own being; it is an enduring and undecaying jar upon a hill in Tennessee. It holds round and shapes forever its share of the general air. Or a book no one is reading is like Victoria Falls, or a zoo at night, its internal activities unperceived. Its virtues are untapped, like those of an empty wall socket. The bright lights of a book no one is reading bounce inside its binding unseen, like the streaking electronic light inside a computer game's screen, which draws its endless patterns in a dark corner of a bar whether someone is watching or no. At any rate, we measure the function and value of human objects in human terms (unless we regard the art object as a natural fact, as the first view above does); so that object's doing, however internal, requires a perceiver to complete its value.

The art object does not do to us; rather, it presents to us. What does it present? It presents an object for study and contemplation. Why should we study and contemplate this object more than any other, more than a pebble or a pelican? After all, the art object wholly lacks certain qualities which we prize. Its components may lack simple material presence—mass and extension—such as we find in the components of pebbles. As a total object, the art object lacks life, the capacity to grow and change and reproduce, spontaneity, mobility, warmth, senses and sensations, appetite, and other such fine things which any pelican possesses. Nevertheless, the art object may represent these things. And in the manner of its representing—in its surface and in its structure—the art object may present, embody, and enact certain additional qualities. We clearly prize these additional qualities as much as, or even more than, we prize the qualities of pebbles and pelicans, or we would never read or sketch on the beach. We find in art objects qualities in which the great world and its parts seem often wanting: human significance, human order, reason, mind, causality, boundary, harmony, perfection, coherence, purity, purpose, and permanence.

In *Fiction and the Figures of Life,* William Gass says, and I concur, "The aim of the artist ought to be to bring into the world objects which do not already exist there, and objects which are especially worthy of love." Always crucial to these thoughts is the caveat that art is lovable and has beauty neither according to its novelty as a newborn object on earth nor according to the lovableness and beauty of the worldly objects it represents, but only according to its internal merits as art. Thus painting has turned from pretty ladies; thus a photographer makes little progress in his art until he ceases making prints of beautiful or lovable objects (like leaves or slaves), the aesthetic or moral virtues of which he attempts to borrow or heist. Similarly, fiction's function is not to people the earth with lovable folk and their dramatic doings in order to widen our acquaintance and cheer our stay on the planet. In *A Dance to the Music of Time*, Anthony Powell manufactures the representation of a person named Kenneth Widmerpool, who is neither beautiful nor lovable. As an artifice, he is both. Graham Greene's *Brighton Rock* is about as crafted a novel as you will find. Its subject, which it presents with unflagging intensity, is human evil. It is very, very good. So also is *Ship of Fools*; so is *The Good Soldier*. As objects, these works possess integrity, intelligence, harmony, and so forth, although their characters and events may not. These points are widely understood; I beg indulgence for mentioning them again.

Art remakes the world according to sense. The art object is a controlled context whose parts cohere within an order according to which they may be understood. Context is meaning. With all my heart, and in vain, I have hoped to avoid or conceal the question of what, if anything, these artistic coherencies have to do with the actual world.

Are the world's artists, with all their noble orderings, playing in the sand? Another way to phrase the same question is this: do artists discover order, or invent it? Do they discern it, or make it up? Finally—are the significance, causality, harmony, purpose, etc., which we find in art objects to be found in the actual world? The remainder of this book devolves upon this question. Are these structures really intelligences, the products of knowledge, which enlighten; or are they instead only play-pretties, the products of wishing, which console?

It is a shame, having stated the question so tidily, and I hope so poignantly, that we must now disallow it. For the drearily abstract truth of the matter is that there is no final difference between the two choices. The question pertains only to the realm of positivist knowledge—to science. One may discover America, which is actual, or invent a unicorn, which is not. Inventing a trip to the moon is mere literature until we discover a way to get there; the discovery of a unicorn would be very hard news indeed. In science, our fictions do not necessarily create our facts (although, as is well known, they may certainly facilitate their discovery, as Kepler's elaborate, angelical cosmology led him to posit elliptical orbits). Even in the sciences, however, the matter becomes steadily cloudier as the levels of abstraction climb. What do we mean by asking if a context is actual? According to whom? For all we know of the actual is our knowledge of it, and that knowledge is contextual, partial, verbal, and so forth. Do we know that the brown pelican, *Pelecanus occidentalis*, is a bird of the order Pelecaniformes and the family Pelecanidae—or did somebody just make that up? Did we discover the calculus or invent it? Do we discover or invent a new move in chess? Did we discover or invent the qualities of color and charm in particles? Antimatter?

Outside of positivism, in the realm of understanding—of human interpretation—invention and discovery are the same process. It is all fiction. Did Plato, or Kant, or Freud, discover a series of significant relationships, or fabricate it? Did Noam Chomsky discover a series of significant relationships, or fabricate it? Did Schönberg? Did Mondrian? Did Confucius or the Baal Shem-Tov discover a series of significant relationships or fabricate it? Did Shakespeare? Did Conrad, did Beethoven, did Donne? The question is meaningless.

But let us go further. The intellectual, interpretative orders which we find in art objects must be there to be found in the actual world, for somebody found them, if only by making them up. But surely there are false interpretations, such as that the Aryan race is destined to rule Europe. Surely there are human orders which only madmen discern, such as the one in which the tide of history is understood to have risen and borne upon its breast the returned general Napoleon Bonaparte, in the person of the speaker. How do we distinguish between those inventions which we honor by the name "discoveries"—such as Freud's—and those inventions we dismiss as balderdash, such as the doctrine of signatures? Alas, we have only empiricism. Some interpretations, such as Plato's and Freud's and Buddha's, are still proving useful in their respective fields. This, in turn, is a matter of consensus. Consensus within various cultures sets useful inventions/discoveries in the shrines of convention, where they reign until consensus changes, when some even more useful fiction replaces the old, as the doctrine of signatures was replaced. This is all very well, and establishes that much of our question is disallowed. But we press on.

What are we to make of artistic interpretations of the

great world? Do they obtain? Do those in what consensus calls a great work obtain in the actual world? We have seen that, so far as we know, interpretations of natural facts do not obtain outside their artistic contexts; Melville has not explained to us whales. Interpretations of *human* facts, however, may well obtain outside their contexts. In the presentation of Achilles and Lear and Lord Jim and Madame Bovary and Dorothea Casaubon and Ahab we may discern relationships between character and event, or character and its parts, which empiricism, if it could ever be directed to such insubstantial ends, would I think discover to be actual recurring patterns. These structures are actual; the articulation of them is discovery. This is a great value of literature. But this is referential. It presents a model of discoveries, of relationships interpreted out of the great world. Well and good.

But please, what about *artistic* (not interpretative) values in art? The idea of order is actual; a pebble is an ordering. But do the ordered relationships among all parts which we find in a great short story or sonnet exist in nature? Do the reflexive structures and intellectual patterns and purpose which we find in art—do these obtain elsewhere? Or do we merely make them up because our minds are uniquely adapted for making things up?

This is an appalling possibility. If our minds are selected for inventing bits of order, then art's highest function is to shed light on the mind. And, terribly, any human artifact is the mind's own simulacrum. A play or a government, a canal or a culture, is a physical replica by means of which the mind duplicates its own structures unwittingly, as a strand of DNA replicates itself inside a banana leaf. And if *this* is true, and the natural world which churned out the mind is a wreck and a chaos, like a rock slide, then the mind is a marvelous monster indeed. And the work of art (in addition to being the least of our worries) is always a tour de force in which the mind displays abilities absurdly in excess of, or at least incidental to, their survival function. For the ability to conceive and execute murals and epic poems and symphonies and novels is a grotesque trick of tissue which sprang from the pot of the possible, like the grossly overdeveloped antlers of the extinct Irish elk.

The mechanism would be this. The overrefined abilities which go into the production of art, religion, and any systems of value would have persisted within the expanding brain of the species, and developed further, and in fact made a rollicking success of the lot of us, because they are extremely adaptive—not for understanding what is, but for getting through the winter. The fictive ability to invent and order makes possible the imaginative conception and execution of shaped tools, the agricultural calendar, complex societies with myth, social ideals, and civic order, and other such dreary, survival-enhancing phenomena. The murals and novels, then, while not specifically useful, would be merely harmless excrescences of the same adaptive tissues, or at best, useful models of social ideals, or abstractly, ideas of order. By these lights, there is no order anywhere but in our brains, which are uniquely adapted for inventing it and for handling complex abstractions. These abilities have served us very well. The only significance and value which obtain anywhere are in the mind's discernment of these fictive qualities in its own manufactured models. We create value and locate it in our monstrously overdeveloped mental self-replication, our stuttering repetitions of our brains' own order, with which we have covered the gibbering earth.

This is the most dismal view—of art and of everything—I can imagine. It must be admitted that one idea in this book is consistent with this view, and even points to it: the suggestion that we already agree tacitly that human significance is the only significance. Although all the generations of people, ever since we can remember—artists, thinkers, cranks, and pagans of every stripe—have intensively sought and sometimes found meaning in the natural world, none of those meanings has "stuck." Nowhere does any consensus agree upon any set of human meanings for the natural world, but only for the human world. Our dwelling places where we dwell, along continental coasts and inland river valleys, are the only sites where what we want and so fiercely imagine can be found, the brain's own baby doll: purpose, significance, and harmony. In the fabrication of these things we are skilled because the skill feeds and preserves us, as the specially adapted tissues of benthic fishes or of dragonflies feed and preserve them. Our brains secrete bright ideas and forms of order; armored scale insects secrete wax from their backs. Thus Cro-Magnon man imagines a long process like dressing skins, like planting grains, like forming diversified societies; thus armored scale insects survive humped under their own goo.

And here we all are. Let us cover this archaeological pit for the nonce and build a high tower. Do we discover reason and harmony in the universe, or do we invent it? Here is another answer to the question, and an entirely jolly one, from contemporary metaphysician Carl Curtis.

By his cheering lights, truth is beauty and beauty truth. Harmony and substance are a spectrum, perhaps hooked in a relationship that can be expressed in words. Einstein's formula may suffice. Curtis says: "Harmony is our one intellectual standard of truth-and-reality; substance (sensory lumpiness) is our felt criterion of worldly actuality.... The *sign* of reality is, to the intellect, harmony; to the body, substantiality." In other words, if it is firm and lumpy we know it is real; and if it is beautiful, we know it is true. (Harmony he defines, with F. H. Bradley, as a property of Absolute Reality concomitant with its coherence, noncontradiction, and pleasure.)

We may wonder what such thinking would make of an excellent novel which shows the final reality to be incoherent, contradictory, painful, and meaningless. Is it true because it is consistent? I can answer for neither Curtis nor Bradley; I suggest, however, timidly and Platonically, that any coherent order is true insofar as it is order, as it partakes of universal order; and some orders are more comprehensive, and more true, than others. At any rate, it is a pity that this argument takes place at a level of abstraction which prevents its being so vivid, and therefore perhaps so convincing, as the gloomy one above.

We have seen that art objects which refer to the world also interpret it, and that these interpretations may be both valid and useful outside the work of art itself. Such an object does something quite definite: it knows and understands, and presents its knowledge and understanding. It may be naive to ask what we can learn from *Othello*, but it is decadent not to. In addition to referring to the world, however, art objects present internally coherent patterns, and some mule-headedness has led us to ask if these ordered patterns are discovered or invented, if they are actual in the great world or only imagined in the human world. After all, our eyes will perceive a tangle of strands in front of a light (such as a pine bough near a street lamp, or fiberglass "angel hair" on a shopping mall Christmas tree) as a perfect circle. But it is illusion. The pine needles and the fiberglass aren't really arranged in perfect circles. It could be, then, that the order we fancy we perceive about us is just such a perceptual trick, a trick by which the mind perceives its own structures, just as a molecule of a certain compound is shaped in such a way that it may combine only with those complementary molecules which match it precisely. A jigsaw puzzle piece can "know" only its neighbors, and is in no position to comment upon the rest of the puzzle.

Or it could be that the order we discern and create is actual. Either we bring it forth by creating it, and so, perhaps, add to the sum of the universe's actual order; or we discern it with our minds and senses and art, generation by generation, discovering bits of the puzzle now here, now there. The art object, in this view, is a cognitive instrument which presents to us, in a stilled and enduring context, a model of previously unarticulated or unavailable relationships among ideas and materials. Insofar as we attend to these art objects, these epistemologically absurd and mysterious hot-air balloons, we deepen our understanding. The order which the artist devises for his fabrications is a chip off the universal order, and partakes of its being. We learn. If we may learn to know, may we not learn to understand? After all, our physical knowledge is, although partial, nevertheless not only adequate but also increasing. Our batting average is nothing short of magnificent; we have cleared the fences and hit the very moon. It could be, then, that our understanding has the capacity, at least, to grow and expand in its realm.

Which shall it be? Do art's complex and balanced relationships among all parts, its purpose, significance, and harmony, exist in nature? Is nature whole, like a completed thought? Is history purposeful? Is the universe of matter significant? I am sorry; I do not know.

Source Notes

Page

28-29   David Sylvester, *Magritte* (New York: Frederick A. Praeger, 1969), pp. 2-3.

37   Witold Gombrowicz, *Ferdydurke/Pornografia/Cosmos*, trans. Eric Mosbacher (New York: Grove Press, 1978), p. 49.

47   Alain Robbe-Grillet, *For a New Novel: Essays on Fiction*, trans. Richard Howard (New York: Grove Press, 1965), p. 33.

56   Arthur Stanley Eddington, *The Nature of the Physical World* (New York: Macmillan, 1933), p. 332.

56   James Jeans, *The Mysterious Universe* (New York: Macmillan, 1931), p. 158.

57   Marcel Proust, *Swann's Way*, trans. C. K. Scott Moncrieff (New York: Vintage Books, 1970), p. 63.

58   Italo Calvino, *Invisible Cities*, trans. William Weaver (New York: Harcourt Brace Jovanovich, 1972).

59   Jorge Luis Borges, "Tlön, Uqbar, Orbis Tertius," *Ficciones*, trans. Anthony Kerrigan (New York: Grove Press, 1962).

72   James Joyce, *Finnegans Wake* (New York: Viking Press, 1939), p. 505.17.

73   Robert Scholes, *Fabulation and Metafiction* (Urbana: University of Illinois Press, 1979), pp. 31-32.

75   "Experience," *The Selected Writings of Ralph Waldo Emerson*, ed. Brooks Atkinson (New York: Random House, 1950), p. 359.

84   Diane Johnson, "Death for Sale," *New York Review of Books*, Dec. 29, 1979, p. 3.

87   Lawrence Alloway, "Notes on Op Art," in *The New Art*, ed. Gregory Battcock (New York: E. P. Dutton, 1966), p. 85.

96   Dore Ashton, *The Unknown Shore: A View of Contemporary Art* (Boston: Little, Brown, 1962), p. 10.

105   John Ruskin, Preface to 2nd ed., *Modern Painters* (New York: E. P. Dutton, 1906), p. xxvii.

105   *Selections from Ralph Waldo Emerson*, ed. Stephen E. Whicher (Boston: Houghton Mifflin, 1960), p. 185.

108   William Gass, *In the Heart of the Heart of the Country and Other Stories* (New York: Harper & Row, 1968), p. 196.

109   Samuel Beckett, *Molloy/Malone Dies/The Unnamable* (New York: Grove Press, 1955), p. 139.

109   Gombrowicz, *Ferdydurke*, p. 138.

109   *Ibid.*, p. 87.

111   John Bákti, "the footnote as medium," *TriQuarterly* 35-1 (Winter 1976), p. 22.

111   Beckett, *Transatlantic Review* 13 (Summer 1963), pp. 6-7.

112-13   William Burroughs, "a distant hand lifted," *Transatlantic Review* 15 (Spring 1964), p. 57.

113   Nik Cohn, *Arfur* (New York: Simon and Schuster, 1970), p. 25.

113   *Ibid.*, p. 63.

117   Borges, *A Personal Anthology*, trans. Anthony Kerrigan (New York: Grove Press, 1967), p. 50.

117   *Two Novels by Robbe-Grillet*, trans. Richard Howard (New York: Grove Press, 1965), p. 142.

117   "Fathers and Sons," *The Short Stories of Ernest Hemingway* (New York: Charles Scribner's Sons, 1953), p. 491.

118   Wright Morris, *Love Affair—A Venetian Journal* (New York: Harper & Row, 1972), p. 38.

118-19   Morris, *Fire Sermon* (New York: Harper & Row, 1971), p. 55.

119   Henry Green, *Living* (London: Hogarth Press, 1964), pp. 160, 124, 222.

119   *Thirteen Stories by Eudora Welty*, ed. Ruth M. Vande Kieft (New York: Harcourt Brace Jovanovich, 1977), p. 147.

120   Anthony Powell, *At Lady Molly's* (London: Heinemann, 1971), p. 153.

120   J. Henri Fabre, *Souvenirs Entomologiques*, cited in Augustin Fabre, *The Life of J. Henri Fabre*, trans. Bernard Miall (New York: Dodd, Mead, 1921), p. 337.

121   *The Variorum Walden*, ed. Walter Harding (New York: Washington Square Press, 1953), p. 143.

124   Robbe-Grillet, *For a New Novel*, p. 44.

127   Octavio Paz, *Marcel Duchamp*, trans. Rachel Phillips and Donald Gardner (New York: Viking Press, 1978), p. 75.

128   Jeffrey Mehlman, *Revolution and Repetition: Marx, Hugo, Balzac* (Berkeley: University of California Press, 1977).

129   Harold Bloom, *The Anxiety of Influence* (New York: Oxford University Press, 1973), p. 95.

132   *Collected Papers of Charles Sanders Peirce*, vol. 5 (Cambridge: Harvard University Press, 1934), p. 157.

134   Martin Gardner, "Mathematical Games," *Scientific American* 242, 2 (Feb. 1980), 14.

137   Hans Prinzhorn, *Artistry of the Mentally Ill*, trans. Eric von Brockdorff (New York: Springer-Verlag, 1972), p. 40.

137   Adolph Wölfli, cited in Roger Cardinal, *Outsider Art* (New York: Praeger, 1972), p. 57.

143   Roger Shattuck, "Painter to the Mind," *New York Times Book Review*, Feb. 11, 1979, p. 13.

157   Saul Bellow, "Leaving the Yellow House," *Mosby's Memoirs and Other Stories* (New York: Viking Press, 1957).

160-62   James Joyce, "The Dead," *Dubliners* (New York: Viking Press, 1967).

163-64   Emile Zola, cited in Charles Child Walcutt, "The Naturalism of Vandover and the Brute," in *Forms of Modern Fiction*, ed. William Van O'Connor (Minneapolis: University of Minnesota Press, 1948), pp. 257-258.

171   Guillaume Apollinaire, "The Cubist Painters," in *Paths to the Present: Aspects of European Thought from Romanticism to Existentialism*, ed. Eugen Weber (New York: Dodd Mead, 1964), p. 233.

176   William Gass, *Fiction and the Figures of Life* (New York: Knopf, 1970), p. 284.

182-83   Carl Curtis, personal letter.

183   F. H. Bradley, *Appearance and Reality*, 2d ed. (New York: Macmillan, 1902), chaps. XIII-XIV.

Index